T0034746

That's
Fact-tastic!

NASA scientists have studied the tufa towers at **Mono Lake** in California, U.S.A., for decades, as similar rock formations are also **found on Mars.**

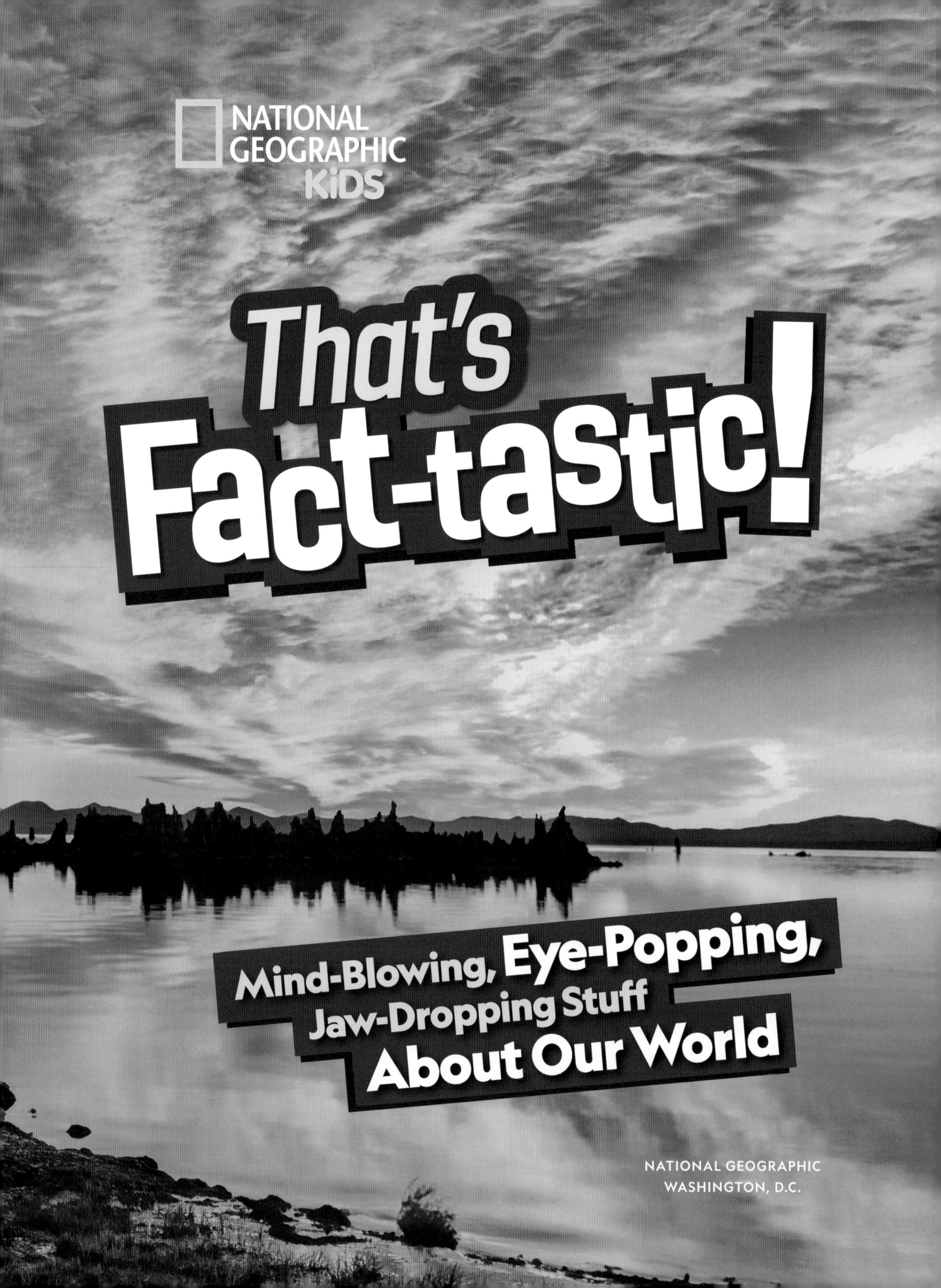
NATIONAL GEOGRAPHIC KIDS
That's Fact-tastic!
Mind-Blowing, Eye-Popping, Jaw-Dropping Stuff About Our World
NATIONAL GEOGRAPHIC
WASHINGTON, D.C.

Contents

6 Amazing Amazon Rainforest Facts

8 Strong Facts About the Human Skeleton

10 Spacecraft Facts That Blast Off

12 What's the Difference?

14 Wondrous Facts About Natural Wonders

16 Earsplitting Facts About Sound

18 Facts About Marine Mammals to Dive Into

20 Basketball Facts You Can Take to the Hoop

22 Awesome Facts About Amphibians

26 Super Sharp Facts About Cheese

28 One Crunchy Fact About Plants

30 Spicy Facts to Make Your Eyes Water

32 Sensational Facts About Seasons

34 Fun Facts About Toys & Games

38 Shipshape Facts About Life on Board

40 Strange Places: Strange Shores

42 Slippery Facts About Cephalopods

44 Wild Facts About Parks and Preserves

46 Festive Facts About Parades

48 Incredible Facts About Inventions

50 Green Facts to Protect the Planet

52 Deep Facts About Canyons

54 Extreme Weirdness

56 Massive Facts About Mega Cities

58 Facts Crawling With Bugs

62 Un-baa-lievable Facts About Barnyard Animals

64 Facts to Calculate About Computer History

66 Freewheeling Facts About Bicycles

68 Facts About Breakfast Foods to Wake You Up

70 Extraordinary Facts About the Future

72 What's the Difference?

74 Surprising Facts About Animals on the Serengeti

76 Powerful Predator Facts

78 Intriguing Facts About Asia

80 Open These Facts About Shells

82 Meaty Facts About Carnivorous Plants

84 Sloth Facts to Hang Out With

86 One Floating Fact About Jellyfish

88 Splashy Facts About Rivers and Lakes

90 Elemental Facts About Elements

92 Holiday Facts to Light Up Your Day

94 Strange Places: The Secrets of Stonehenge

96 Brilliant Facts About the Color Blue

98 Snack on Tasty Facts About Cookies

100 Nighttime Facts About Nocturnal Animals

102 Funky Facts That Will Gross You Out

104 Pirate Facts That Will Shiver Your Timbers

106 Extreme Weirdness

108 Bright Facts About Black Holes

110 Check Into These Facts About Cool Hotels

112 High-Flying Facts About Birds of Prey

114 Colorful Facts About Coral Reefs

118 Get a Kick Out of These Soccer Facts

120 Naturally Pricey Facts

122 Surprising Facts About the Solar System

124 Say G'Day to Awesome Facts About Australia

126 Facts That Will Stick With You

128 What's the Difference?

130 Moving Facts About Migration

132 Facts About Rulers Who Reigned Supreme

134 Exceptional Facts About Elephants

136 Gold Rush Facts to Dig Into

138 Sharp and Stinging Facts About Animal Defenses

140 Ancient Facts About Pyramids

142 Mind-Blowing Facts About Biomimicry

144 Strange Places: Blue Volcano

146 Penguin Facts in Black and White

148 Terrific Facts About Turning Trash Into Treasure

150 Perplexing Facts About Puzzles and Codes

152 Catchy Facts About Famous Musicians

154 Zany Facts About Zoos

156 Dig These Facts About Fossils

158 Extreme Weirdness

160 Facts About Famous Firsts

162 Rev Your Engine With These Facts About Vehicles

164 What's the Difference?

166 Odd Facts About Hoofed Animals

168 Baseball Facts That Hit It Out of the Park

170 Engaging Facts About Europe

172 One Great Gray Seal Fact

174 Cinematic Facts About the Silver Screen

176 Precious Facts About Presidential Pets

178 Prickly Facts That Stick Out

180 One Whispering Whale Fact

182 Behind the Facts

182 Illustration Credits

184 Index

Amazing Amazon Rainforest Facts

1

The **harpy eagle,** which preys on monkeys and sloths, has **talons** larger than a **grizzly bear's** claws.

2

The **toco toucan** can adjust blood flow into its **large bill,** allowing the bird to **keep cool** in the tropical heat.

3

Capybara, the world's **largest rodents,** look like their **guinea pig** relatives but are the size of a **Saint Bernard.**

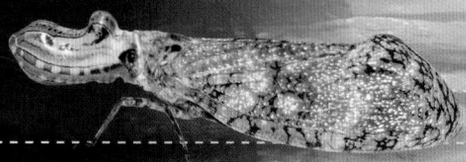

4

The **peanut-head bug,** which lives on the Amazon **forest floor,** has a **head** that looks like an unshelled **peanut.**

5

A **glass frog's** belly is **see-through,** so you can see its **heart beating.**

6

The Amazon rainforest is **twice the size** of India.

7

Some parts of the Amazon get **400 inches** (1,016 cm) of **rainfall** a year.

8

After seasonal rains, the **Amazon River** floods forests, allowing freshwater Amazon river dolphins to swim **among the trees.**

9

The green anaconda, the **world's heaviest snake,** weighs more than a **mountain gorilla.**

10

The Amazon is so **dense with vegetation** that it can take **10 minutes** for **rain** to **reach the ground.**

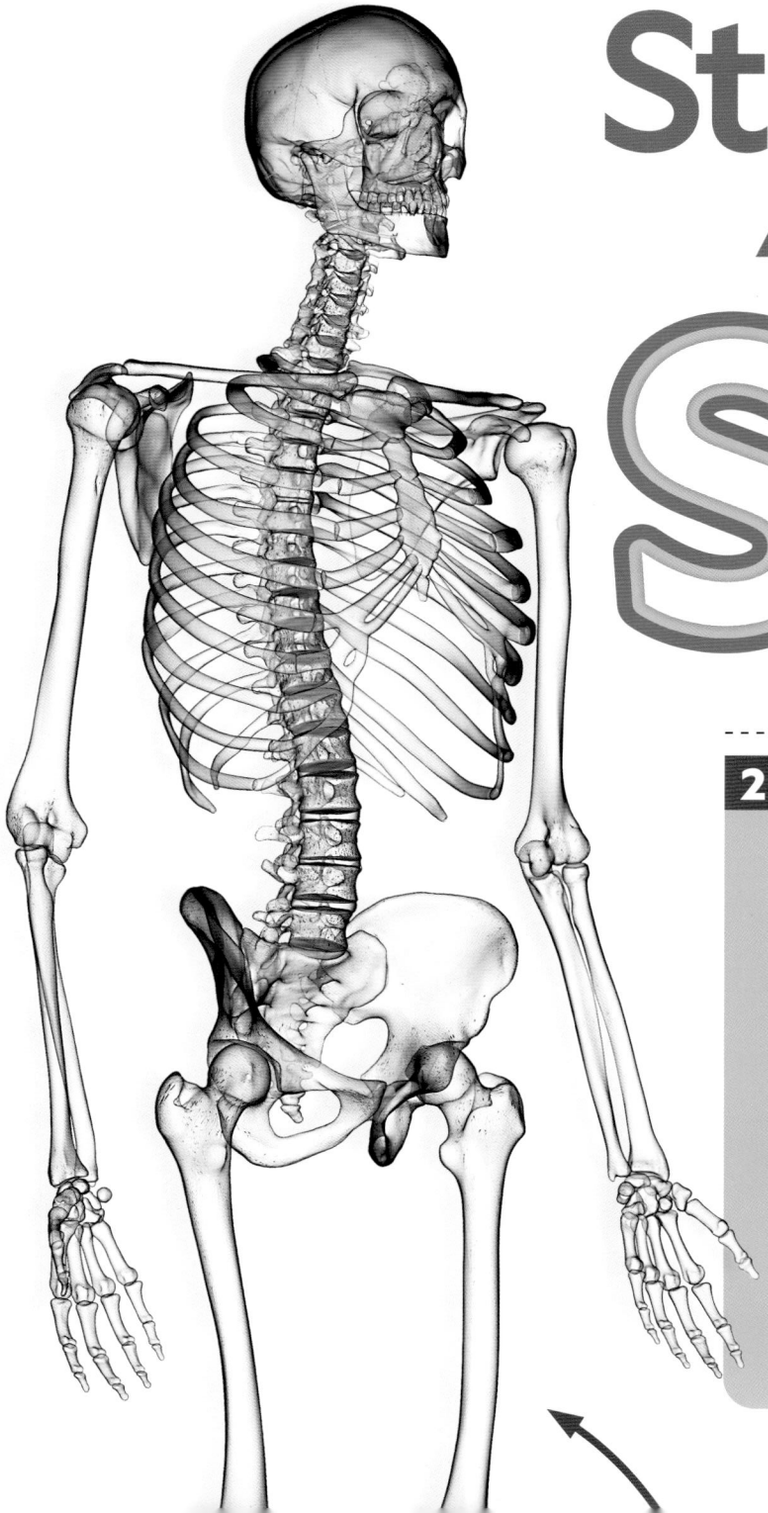

Strong Facts About the Human Skeleton

1 The bone that kids most commonly break is the collarbone.

2 Babies have about 100 more bones than adults. (Some bones fuse together as a baby grows.)

3 Most of an adult's skeleton regenerates every 10 years—new bone grows to replace the old.

4

The **thighbone** is the **longest and strongest** bone in the body.

5

The **funny bone** isn't actually a bone— **it's a nerve** that runs inside your elbow.

6

The average **adult skeleton** weighs **20 pounds** (9 kg).

7

The bones in your **hands and wrists** make up about **a quarter** of all the bones in your body.

8

The **smallest bone** in your body, located in **your middle ear,** is about **half as long** as a grain of rice.

9

The hyoid is the **only bone** in your body **not connected** to another one— it's located at the **base of your tongue.**

10

Teeth are part of the **skeletal system,** and the enamel that covers them is **stronger than bone.**

Spacecraft

Facts That Blast Off

1

Astronauts on the International Space Station season their food with liquid salt and pepper—grains might float away and clog the air vents.

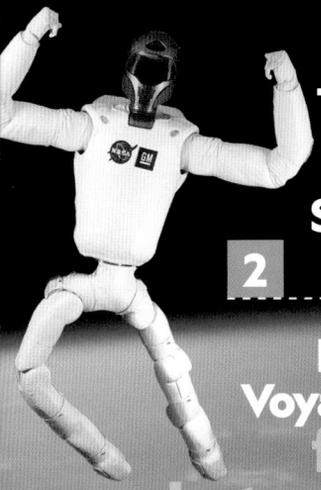

The legs of Robonaut 2, a **humanoid robot** designed to work **alongside astronauts** on the International Space Station, are **nine feet** (2.7 m) long when fully extended.

2

3

In 1990, Voyager 1 took the **first and only photograph** of our **solar system.**

4

Sleeping bags on the International Space Station are **tied to the walls** so that the astronauts won't float around the room while they sleep.

5

In 2018, the spacecraft company SpaceX **launched** a **red convertible car** into space.

6

During its **nine years in space,** the Kepler Space Telescope **discovered** more than **2,600 planets** outside our solar system.

7

The **space shuttle** can go from zero to **17,000 miles an hour** (27,360 km/h) in 8.5 minutes—that's **100 times faster** than the **fastest race cars.**

8

On its final flybys of the sun in 2025, the **Parker Solar Probe,** a spacecraft sent to gather data about the **sun's surface,** will travel 430,000 miles an hour (692,000 km/h)—fast enough to get from Tokyo, Japan, to New York, U.S.A., in **less than a minute.**

9

Mars rovers practice for their missions in Chile's **Atacama Desert** because that's the place on Earth most similar to **Mars.**

10

The Mars rover Perseverance is looking for **signs that life**—in the form of microbes—**once existed** on the **red planet.**

What's the Difference?

Check out these similar pairings and see how you can determine this from that!

BISON VS. BUFFALO

The confusion begins with the lyrics of the classic folk song about the American West, "Home on the Range": "Oh, give me a home, where the buffalo roam / Where the deer and the antelope play ..." Here's the problem: There aren't any buffalo in the United States. Water buffalo live in South Asia, and African buffalo live in Africa. It's actually the American bison that lives in the United States. European explorers likely started the mix-up by misnaming North America's heaviest land animal. But an American bison and a buffalo won't win any look-alike contests. For starters, bison have a telltale hump on their shoulders and buffalo do not. This hump serves bison well in snowy weather, when they use their hump and their head to plow snow and graze the grasses beneath. For another clue, look no further than the crescent-shaped horns on a buffalo's head. They can grow up to six feet (1.8 m) long! Bison horns are shorter and are used to defend the animals against predators ... on the range.

Water buffalo

INSECT VS. ARACHNID VS. BUG

Not all "bugs" are *really* bugs. Scientists categorize these creatures into three different groups: insects, arachnids, and true bugs. Here's how to sort them out. Insect bodies have three parts: a head, a middle section (called a thorax), and an abdomen. They have a hard external skeleton, or exoskeleton, and antennae, and adults have six legs. At some point in their life, most insects have wings. Bees, beetles, flies, and wasps are all insects. Arachnids are quite different from insects. Arachnid bodies have only two sections, an abdomen and a combined head and thorax. They have neither antennae nor wings, and they have eight legs. Spiders, scorpions, and ticks are arachnids. A "true bug" is a type of insect, but not all insects are true bugs. The main thing that separates a true bug from other insects is its mouth. True bugs include aphids, bedbugs, and stink bugs.

Stinkbug

HIKING VS. TREKKING

Hiking and trekking are both great ways to get outside and explore the world on foot. So why are there two names for taking a walk? The terms overlap a little, but don't let the differences trip you up. Hiking usually means walking in the woods or on trails. A hike might last for several hours, and you can take one on a moment's notice—just lace up your boots, fill up your water bottle, and head for the trails. Trekking, on the other hand, involves a few more steps. A trek often lasts several days. It requires more planning and more gear. But many people use the word "hike" for both types of walking adventures. A hike can be as long and as challenging as a trek. The word "trek," however, isn't often used for a short stroll in the woods.

LEGEND VS. MYTH

Once upon a time ... Two of the oldest types of stories are legends and myths. Legends are usually based on a real person or event. However, the story often changes and the facts become exaggerated. Tales of brave people and extraordinary deeds are told and retold for many years. Soon, the story—the legend—is bigger than the person or event that inspired it. Stories about King Arthur and Robin Hood are legends based on real people (who may not have been much like their legendary characters at all). Myths, on the other hand, aren't based on real people or events. They are often stories made up to explain things people didn't understand well, such as how the world came to be or why birds can fly. Unlike legends, which are about humans, myths are usually about gods or other supernatural creatures. The stories of Greek gods, goddesses, and heroes are examples of myths.

SORBET VS. SHERBET

A big scoop of cold, fruity sorbet or sherbet makes a refreshing, sweet treat on a hot summer day. You may not care which your bowl holds, as long as it melts in your mouth, but these two frozen desserts are different. Sorbet is made with only fruit and sugar. This keeps the treat yummy but light. Sherbet is a little richer and creamier. It has fruit and sugar, too, but also a small amount of milk or cream and maybe some eggs or gelatin. Now when you visit the snack stand at the beach, you'll know just what's in your favorite scoop.

Sorbet

STAR VS. PLANET

When you look up at the night sky, you see a sprinkling of glowing lights. Many of these are stars, but some are planets. What's the difference? A star is a giant ball of flaming gases, mostly hydrogen and helium. Inside a star, hydrogen atoms and helium atoms collide, or bump into each other. These collisions create a huge amount of energy. This energy is what makes a star glow. More than 100 billion stars twinkle in our galaxy, the Milky Way. Stars make their own light, but planets don't—they can only reflect light from stars. Planets move in a fixed orbit around a star, and in our solar system, that star is the sun. So when you see a planet in the night sky, it appears to glow because it is reflecting light from the sun. But how can you tell a star from a planet when you're looking at the sky from Earth? Stars twinkle. Planets don't.

Wondrous Facts About Natural Wonders

1

The **northern lights** make sounds—described as crackles or **muffled bangs**—that can be heard from the ground.

2

You can **hear** the rushing water of **Victoria Falls** from a mile (1.6 km) away.

Dead Sea

3

The **Eye of the Sahara**, a **geological formation** that can be seen from space, is sometimes **used as a landmark** by **astronauts**.

4

The **Dead Sea** is **not totally dead**—fish and plants can't survive, but **bacteria, algae, and fungi** thrive.

5

The **giant sequoias** in California, U.S.A., are **resistant** to disease and can live up to **3,000 years.**

6

The **Great Barrier Reef** covers about the same area as **70 million soccer fields.**

7

Split Apple Rock, or Tokangawhā, is a 120-million-year-old granite **boulder** off the coast of New Zealand that may have been used as an ancient astronomical **calendar.**

8

Wind speeds at the summit of **Mount Everest** can be **stronger** than those in a category 5 **hurricane.**

9

The Galápagos Islands have been called a **"living museum"** because of the **unique animals** found there, such as the **giant tortoise.**

10

There's **one town** inside the **Grand Canyon** in Arizona, U.S.A.—it can only be reached by **hiking, riding an animal,** or flying in **by helicopter.**

1

Sound waves travel faster underwater than they do through the air.

2

On the Supreme Scream ride at Knott's Berry Farm in California, U.S.A., riders experience three seconds of weightlessness as they drop at 50 miles an hour (80 km/h).

3

Dogs don't always say "woof": In Iceland they say "voff," and in Romania it's "ham."

4

The 1980 eruption of Mount St. Helens in Washington State, U.S.A., was heard more than 200 miles (322 km) away.

5

A black hole in the Perseus Cluster, some 250 million light-years away, "hums" a sound about one million billion times lower than any human can hear.

6

To make sure cars could hear him as he biked, a man in London, England, invented the Hornster, a horn louder than a jet engine.

7

Cicadas create their loud buzzing by "buckling" two tymbals, organs on their exoskeletons, like an accordion.

Earsplitting Facts About Sound

8

A **pet cat** named Merlin **once purred** about **as loud as a vacuum cleaner.**

9

Male white **bellbirds,** which live in the Amazon rainforest, can **sing as loud** as an **ambulance siren.**

10

Elephants make **low rumbles** in their throats that travel for about **3.5 miles** (5.6 km) underground and are so strong that humans can **feel the vibrations.**

A baby dugong—a relative of manatees—may catch a ride on its mother's back.

1

2

Harp seals get their name from the harp-shaped ring on the adults' backs.

3

Beluga whales rub up against rocks to shed their skin.

4

When harbor porpoises come up for air, they make a puffing noise that sounds like a sneeze.

5

Walruses have air sacs in their necks that act like life preservers to help them float.

6

A newborn otter's extra-thick fur makes it impossible for the little one to sink.

7

The lungs of the sperm whale are designed to collapse to withstand the pressure of its deep dives.

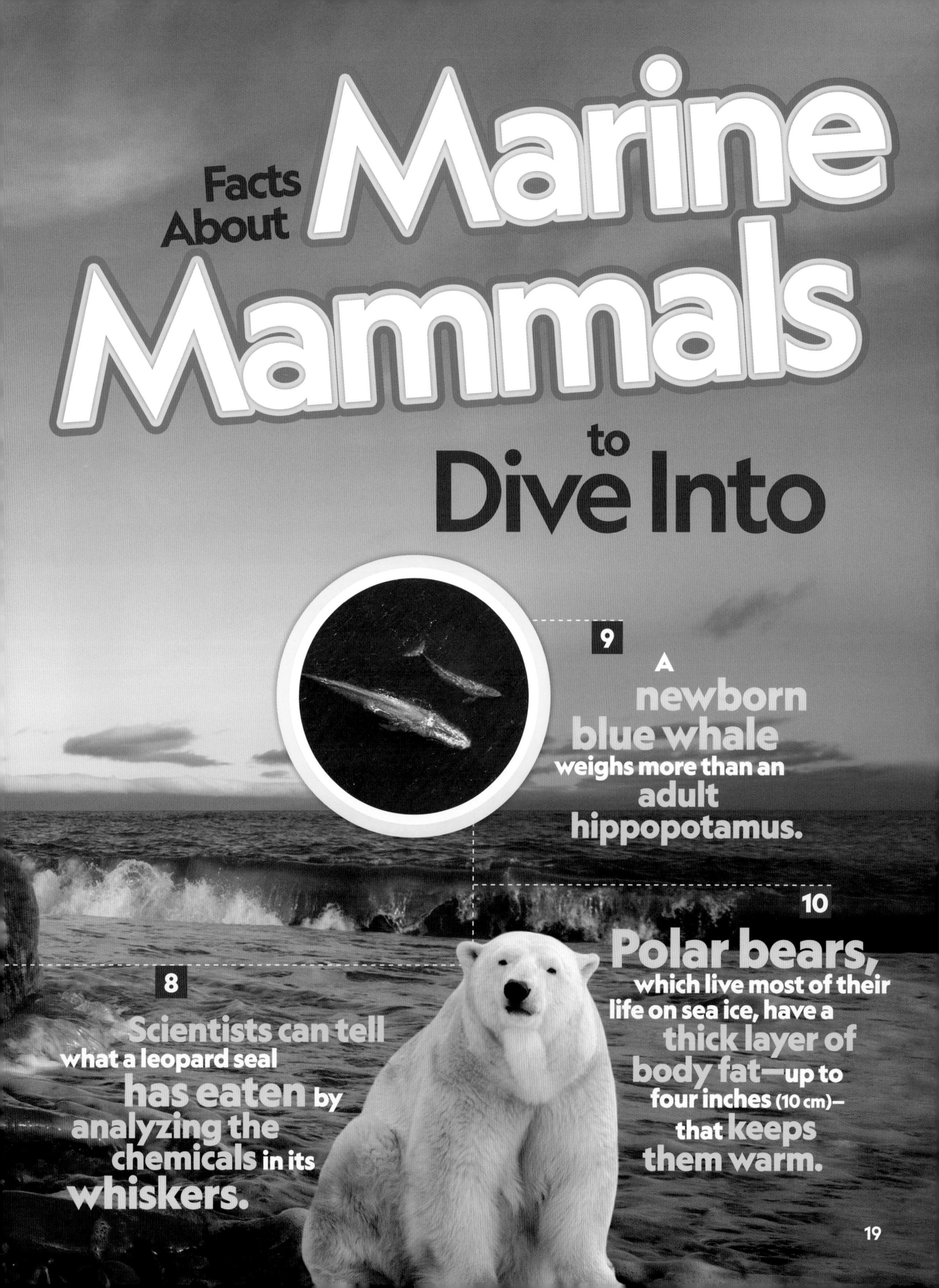

Facts About Marine Mammals to Dive Into

9

A newborn blue whale weighs more than an adult hippopotamus.

10

Polar bears, which live most of their life on sea ice, have a thick layer of body fat—up to four inches (10 cm)—that keeps them warm.

8

Scientists can tell what a leopard seal has eaten by analyzing the chemicals in its whiskers.

Basketball Facts You Can Take to the Hoop

1

The U.S. Supreme Court building has a basketball court on the top floor.

2

The NBA's Philadelphia 76ers got their name because the Declaration of Independence was signed in the city in 1776.

3

Golden State Warrior Stephen Curry has been fined $100 by his mom for each turnover he makes after his third in a game.

4

Former NBA star Shaquille O'Neal wears size 22 shoes.

A warm basketball is bouncier than a cold one.

7

5

Basketball was first played using soccer balls.

6

The first basketball hoops were peach baskets.

The longest successful basketball shot measured 112 feet 6 inches (34.3 m), longer than the entire length of a court.

8

9

Regardless of experience, American men have a 17 percent chance of playing for the NBA if they are 7 feet (2 m) or taller.

10

Dribbling was not originally part of the game—players could only move the ball by passing it.

Awesome Facts About Amphibians

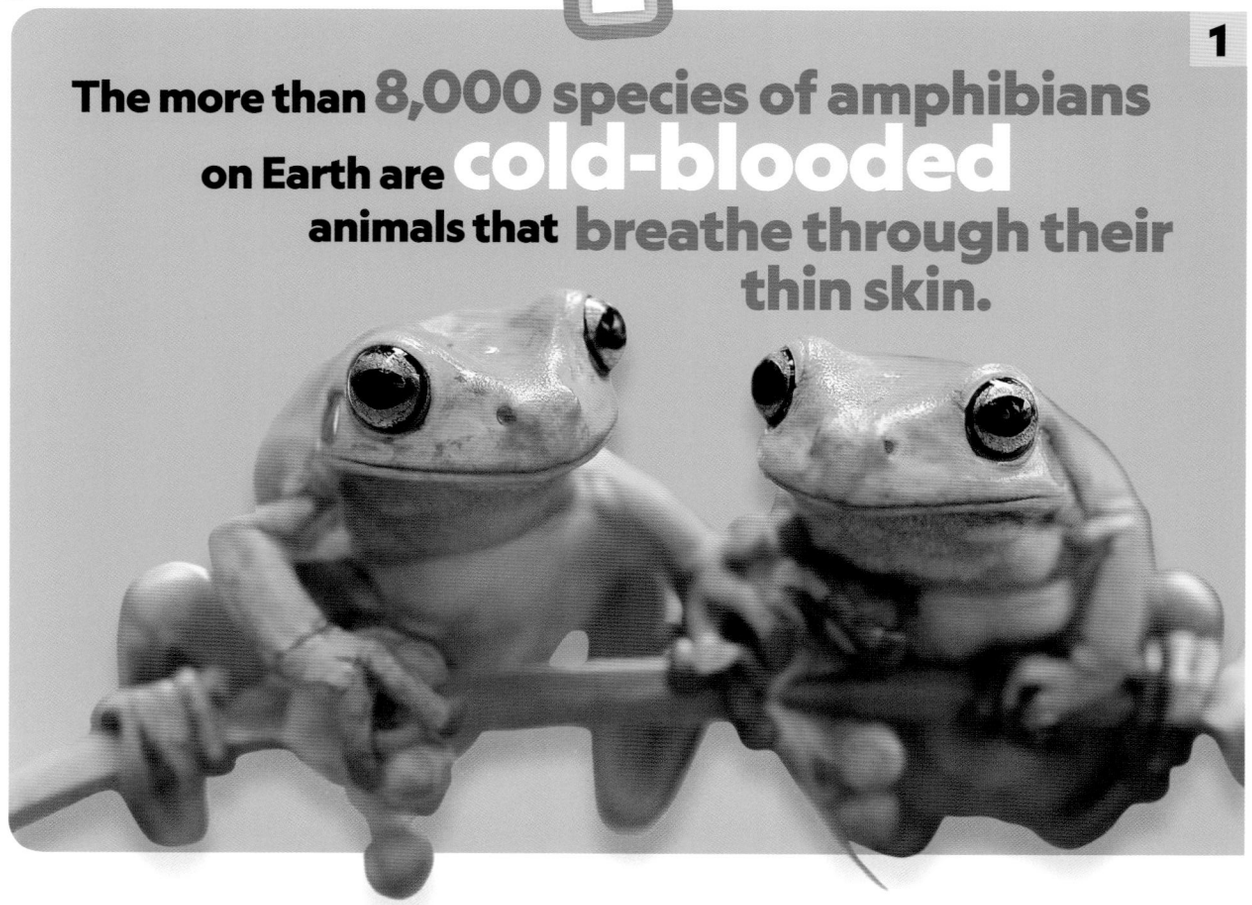

1

The more than 8,000 species of amphibians on Earth are cold-blooded animals that breathe through their thin skin.

2

Mexican axolotls (ACK-suh-LAH-tuhls), a kind of salamander, can regrow lost body parts.

3

Skin almost completely **covers the eyes** of some **underground caecilian** (sih-SIL-yen) species.

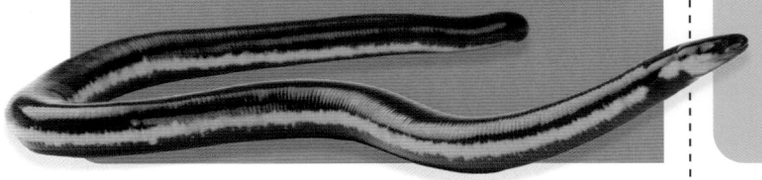

4

The **world's largest caecilian** lives in Colombia and grows to be nearly **five feet** (1.5 m) **long**—that's taller than the average **11-year-old.**

5

Tadpoles have **tiny teeth** they use to eat pond plants.

6

The word **"amphibian"** comes from the Greek words for **"both kinds of life,"** since most live part of their life in **water** and part on **land.**

7

Poison frogs belong to the family Dendrobatidae, which means **"tree-walker"** in Latin.

8

About the size of a **bowling ball,** the **armored devil toad** lived alongside the **dinosaurs** and weighed a whopping 10 pounds (4.5 kg).

9

Some people think the **squeaky sound** made by salamanders known as **mudpuppies** is similar to a **dog's bark.**

10

Amphibian teeth are used to **hold prey** but **not to chew it**—amphibians swallow their food **whole.**

Turn the page for more amazing amphibian facts!

11

African clawed frogs can **stay in the mud** at the bottom of **dried-out ponds** for a year **while waiting** for the rains to return.

12

A study found that olms, **aquatic salamanders** that live in **flooded caves** in Bosnia and Herzegovina, **move just a few feet** over several years.

13

The Siberian newt can **hibernate in frozen ground** because it produces **special chemicals** that protect it from **extreme cold.**

14

A **giant cane toad** found in Australia was nicknamed **"Toadzilla"** because it was about the size of a **small dog.**

15

Caecilians are the **only amphibians** with **tentacles.**

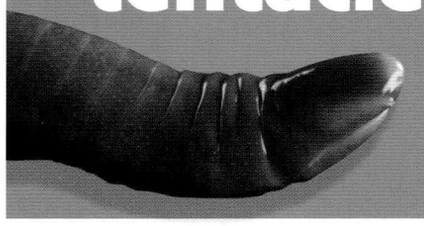

16

A **small tail** is still visible on **froglets**—an intermediary stage **between tadpole** and **adult** frog.

17

Great crested newts, which live only in Europe, produce a **foul-smelling, milky substance** to keep **predators away.**

18

The Great Basin spadefoot, a type of toad, has **hardened tissue** on its **hind feet** that it uses to **dig into the ground** for shelter.

19

Four **small rainforest frogs** that lived about **99 million years ago** were found **preserved in amber** in Myanmar.

20

Poisonous mantella frogs—small, **brightly colored frogs** found only on the island of Madagascar—**get their toxins** from the flies, ants, and termites they eat.

Super Sharp Facts About Cheese

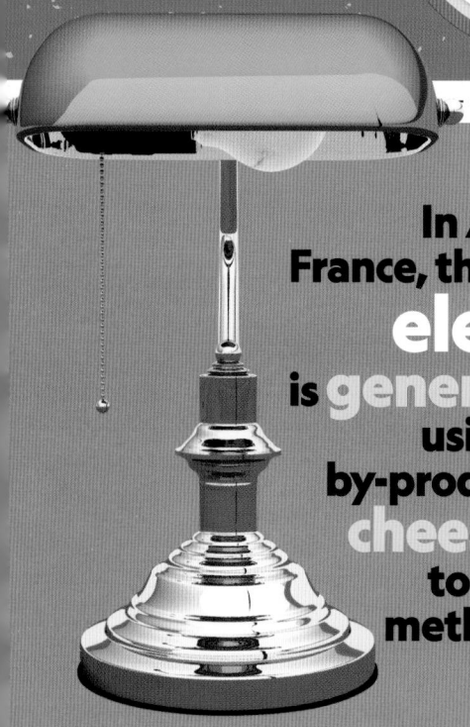

1

In Albertville, France, the town's **electricity** is **generated** by using whey—a by-product of **cheesemaking**—to produce methane gas.

2

It takes about **five quarts** (4.7 L) of **cow's or goat's milk** to make one pound (0.5 kg) of **cheese.**

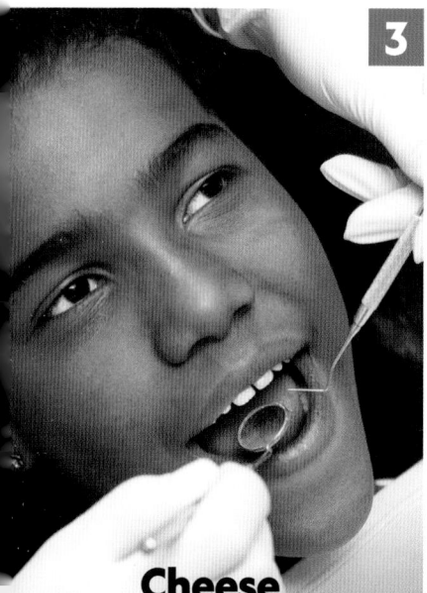

3

Cheese may help prevent cavities.

4

Some **cheeses** are treated with **edible mold** to help them **develop flavor.**

5

In 1835, a dairy farmer gave President Andrew Jackson a 1,400-pound (635-kg) cheese that was said to have remained in the White House for two years.

6

A law in Wisconsin, U.S.A., once required restaurants to serve cheese with meals.

7

The cartoon characters Wallace and Gromit created a boom in international sales of the British cheese Wensleydale because Wallace liked it so much.

8

You can make cheese from nuts.

9

Scientists have made cheese using bacteria taken from human toes and belly buttons.

10

The holes in Swiss cheese are called eyes.

Certain cabbage-like plants **feel the vibrations** of an animal **chewing** on their leaves and **release a chemical** to fend off the creature.

Spicy Facts to Make Your Eyes Water

1

Kimchi, a spicy Korean dish, was originally made by letting **vegetables age** over the winter in earthen pots buried **in the ground.**

2

The **extremely hot** pepper named **Pepper X** is more than **1,200 times hotter** than a jalapeño.

3

The ancient Aztec ruler **Montezuma** reportedly drank more than 50 cups a day of ***xocoatl,*** a **chocolate drink** sometimes flavored with **chili peppers.**

4

Products made from capsaicin—which gives chili peppers their spice—are used to keep deer, voles, and birds away from gardens and crops.

5

A chili pepper's heat is given in units that measure how much sugar water to add to a pepper's oil until you can't taste its heat.

6

Sriracha hot sauce is named for the coastal city of Si Racha, Thailand, where the sauce was first made.

7

Scientists created the Dragon's Breath pepper not to eat but to add to a pain-relieving skin cream.

8

You can taste garlic with your feet.

9

Hot sauce was first advertised for sale in the United States in 1807, and today more than $1.5 billion of the spicy condiment is sold every year.

10

Since people have different numbers of taste buds, spicy foods can taste hotter to one person than to another.

1

In a study of 500 people, a researcher found that **the more time** spent **outdoors** on a sunny day in spring, **the happier** the subjects said they felt.

2

People visit the **Temple of the Sun** and the **Temple of the Moon** outside Mexico City, Mexico, to celebrate the **spring equinox**, when the sun aligns with the Equator.

3

In the fall, a **special layer of cells** forms on **tree leaf stems**, cutting off nutrients to the leaves and causing them to eventually **fall.**

4

The phrase **"dog days of summer"** comes from the ancient Greeks and Romans, who **thought that Sirius** (known as the dog star), which rises before the sun in late July, added a little **extra heat** to the sun.

5

If Earth wasn't **tilted on its axis**, there would be **minor** temperature changes throughout the year but **no seasons.**

Sensational Facts About Seasons

6

In Tromsø, Norway, located about 200 miles (322 km) north of the Arctic Circle, the **sun doesn't rise** from November to January.

7

The ancient Egyptians **divided the year** into **three seasons** based on the Nile: when the **river flooded,** when farmers **planted crops,** and when the crops were **harvested.**

8

In early Anglo-Saxon cultures, **age was counted** by **how many winters** you lived through.

9

During the annual **monsoon season** in the tropics, some **mice "hitch" rides** on the **back of frogs** so that they don't get caught in floods.

10

Seasons on Uranus last for about **21 Earth years.**

Fun Facts About Toys & Games

1

Ancient Greeks used what we now call **Hula-Hoops** as a form of **exercise.**

2

In 1993, **Tetris** became the first **video game in space** when Russian cosmonaut Aleksandr Serebrov played it on the Mir space station.

3

The United States National Security Agency once **banned Furbies** from its offices because it was thought the talking toys might **leak classified information.**

4

Play-Doh was invented in the 1930s to help **clean soot** left by coal-burning **furnaces** off household walls.

5

During **World War II,** the British government sent money, compasses, files, and maps hidden in **Monopoly games** to help their soldiers **escape** from German **prisoner of war** camps.

6

The Little Tikes **Cozy Coupe** toy car **has often outsold** some of the most popular **real cars.**

7

Barbie's full name is **Barbara Millicent Roberts.**

8

McDonald's is the world's largest **toy distributor.**

9

The original **Mr. Potato Head,** created in the United States in 1952, came with eyes, arms, legs, and a mustache—but you had to **provide the potato.**

10

The biggest **Hot Wheels track loop** ever built was **12 feet 8 inches** (3.86 m) **tall.**

Turn the page for more fun facts!

11

A Rubik's Cube has **43 quintillion** possible combinations.

12

In Denmark, a contest offered a **lucky winner** the chance to spend the night in a **house made entirely of Legos.**

13

U.S. soldiers **used Slinkys** as **radio antennas** during the Vietnam War.

14

A **cardboard box** was **inducted** into the U.S. National **Toy Hall of Fame** in 2005.

15

A company sold an **edible version** of **Candy Land**—the playing cards were **made of chocolate.**

16

Worn-down Crayola crayons are called leftolas.

17

Ancient Egyptian kids played a game called Knucklebones that was similar to jacks—they threw sheep toe bones in the air and tried to catch them.

18

A wooden spinning top was found in King Tut's tomb.

19

A NASA engineer invented the Super Soaker after a prototype for a spacecraft's heat pump sprang a leak.

20

Astronauts onboard Apollo 8 used Silly Putty to hold down tools in zero gravity.

Shipshape Facts About Life On Board

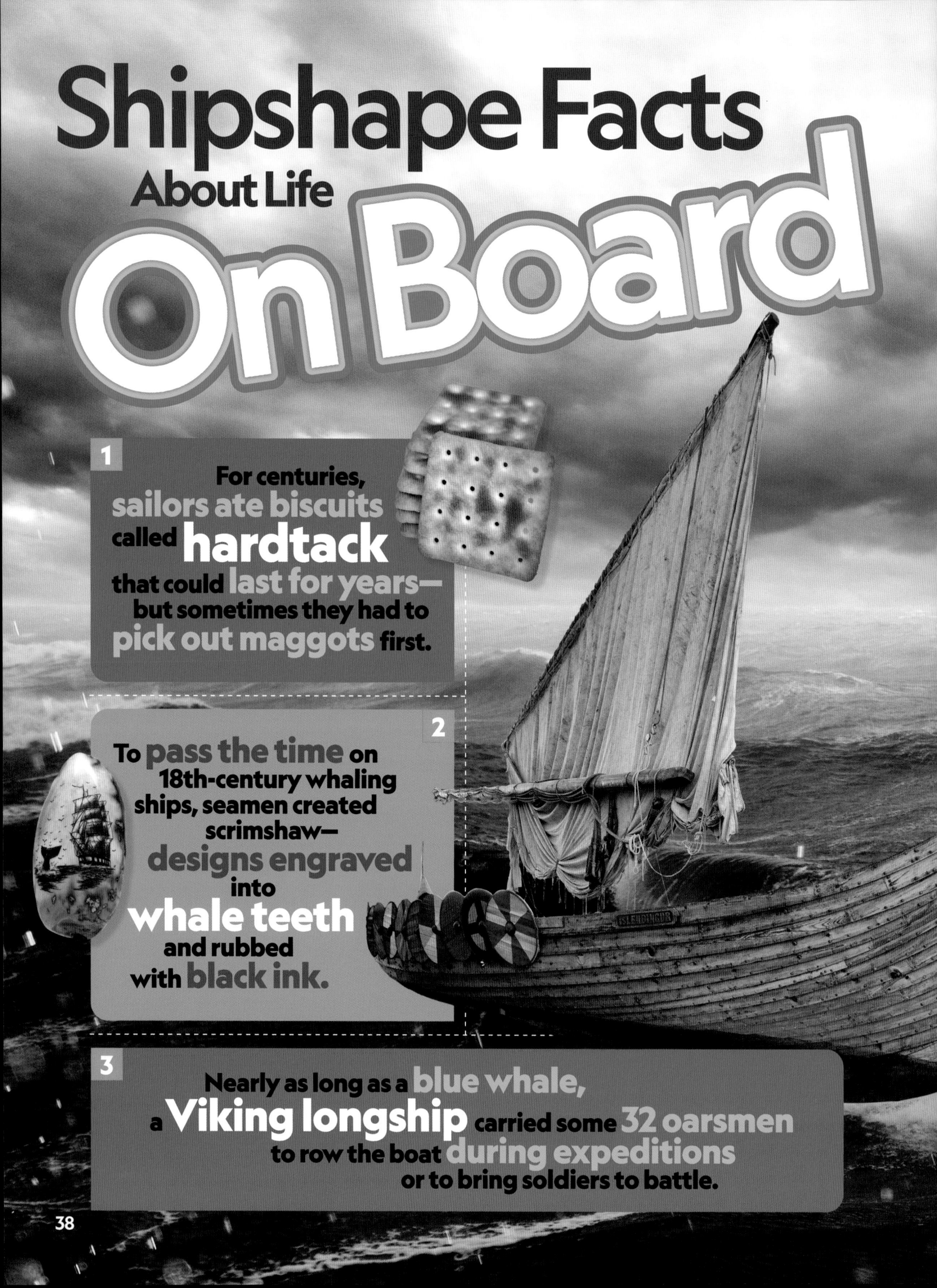

1

For centuries, sailors ate biscuits called **hardtack** that could last for years—but sometimes they had to pick out maggots first.

2

To pass the time on 18th-century whaling ships, seamen created scrimshaw—designs engraved into **whale teeth** and rubbed with black ink.

3

Nearly as long as a blue whale, a **Viking longship** carried some 32 oarsmen to row the boat during expeditions or to bring soldiers to battle.

4

Early sailors sang rhythmic **sea shanties** to help **ease the dullness** of **repetitive tasks** on board.

5

When there are **more people than bunks** on a ship, sailors take turns sleeping in the **same bed,** a practice known as hot bunking or **hot racking.**

6

Nuclear submarines are **so cramped** that spaces often serve **two purposes:** The officers' dining room is a makeshift **hospital,** and the torpedo room is the **workout room.**

7

Sailors used to plug **leaks** with sections of **old rope mixed with tar.**

8

In the late 1600s, sailors went to the bathroom on **"seats of ease"** located on either side of a ship's bow—their waste **dropped through pipes** down into the water.

9

Naturalist **Charles Darwin's** H.M.S. *Beagle* was so **crowded** that he slept in a hammock strung above a drafting table.

10

In 1753, Scottish naval surgeon James Lind showed that **drinking lemon** and **orange juice** could **prevent scurvy,** a disease caused by a vitamin deficiency and often suffered by sailors on long voyages.

Weird water, freaky flies, and mysterious towers rise up in Mono Lake.

Strange gray towers rise from a desert lake reaching skyward like clusters of stout trees. These odd structures may look like living things, but they're not—they're rock formations that "grew" in Mono Lake in California, U.S.A. And they're not the only strange things in the weird water of this curious lake.

ODD AQUATIC LIFE

The lake's salt and natural chemicals make its water inhospitable for fish and other common aquatic creatures, but it's still packed with bizarre life. Trillions of tiny brine shrimp about the size of your fingernail make the lake look like a giant bowl of shrimp soup. Just as abundant—and even weirder—are Mono Lake's freaky alkali flies. They can surround themselves with an air pocket that allows them to "scuba dive" underwater to feed on algae and lay their eggs. The eggs hatch as larvae, which feed underwater. Eventually each larva encases itself in a pupa to change into an adult fly. When it's ready to emerge from its hard pupa, its head splits apart, and a balloonlike structure inside inflates to blow open the pupa. Then its head reassembles, and the adult fly floats to the surface. Mono Lake has more life living in it than most freshwater lakes, and hungry birds know it. Some nest near the all-you-can-eat buffet of shrimp and flies, while migrating birds like phalaropes make pit stops to refuel before their 3,000-mile (4,828-km)-long migration to South America.

WET AND WEIRD

Birds love the brine shrimp, but they won't find any fish in Mono Lake. The lake's nearly three times saltier than the ocean and has an extremely high pH level—a measure of how acidic or alkaline something is. Lifeguards keep the pH level in pools at about seven on the pH scale—to help keep swimmers' eyes comfortable. Mono Lake, which is very alkaline (the opposite of acidic), measures about 10, which is high. "In terms of its pH level, it's a lot like glass cleaner," says Bartshé Miller, education director of the Mono Lake Committee. It might be deadly for fish, but for human swimmers Mono Lake is safe—and weird. The lake water is so loaded with minerals that people float like corks. "It's pretty amazing," Miller says. "You could read a book floating on your back." Swimmer, beware though: The water has a bitter taste and feels greasy.

TOWERING BELOW

The rocky towers that today appear above water originally formed underwater. Freshwater springs gurgling up from the bottom carry calcium, which reacts with the carbonate in the lake water and creates tufa, a kind of rock that contains a lot of calcium carbonate. As the springs flow, the resulting tufa gradually grows. Decades later the tufa becomes a tower as tall as 30 feet (9 m). Groups of tufa towers are visible above the surface because Mono Lake's water level has gone down since they formed.

SAVING A LAKE

Mono Lake may seem like an eco-wasteland, but it's actually an environmental success story. In the 1940s the city of Los Angeles began using some of the water that supplies Mono Lake, and the water level dropped dangerously low. "If the diversion of water continued, Mono Lake would have become a kind of chemical puddle with no life in it," Miller says. But in the 1990s, Los Angeles agreed to use less water to keep Mono Lake alive. "This is a place where the idea of protecting the environment was balanced with the needs of a city," Miller says. "That doesn't always happen, but we achieved it here."

HOW MONO LAKE FORMED

Streams feed Mono Lake, but no water flows out. Over hundreds of thousands of years, evaporation caused minerals carried in by that water to accumulate. Those minerals mixed with ash from nearby erupting volcanoes, creating a unique water chemistry. As the climate warmed after the last ice age, the lake evaporated even more, exposing the rocky towers.

Violet-green swallow

Brine shrimp

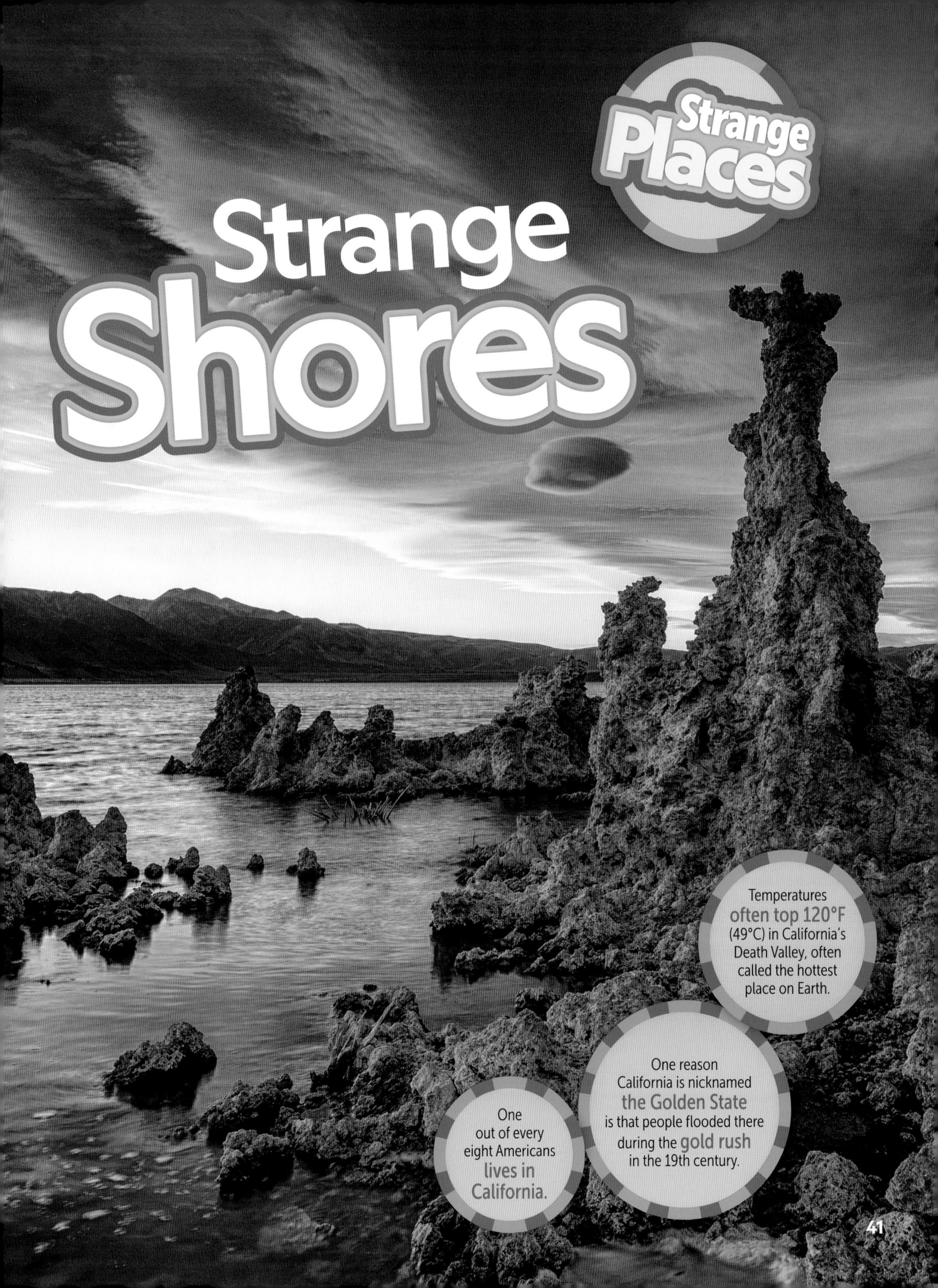

Strange Places

Strange Shores

Temperatures **often top 120°F** (49°C) in California's Death Valley, often called the hottest place on Earth.

One reason California is nicknamed **the Golden State** is that people flooded there during the **gold rush** in the 19th century.

One out of every eight Americans **lives in California.**

1

Scientists **thought octopuses were solitary,** until they discovered massive underwater dens built with shells, which they nicknamed **"Octopolis"** and **"Octlantis."**

2

A single **octopus sucker** can **lift 35 pounds** (16 kg).

3

Octopuses have **brain cells** in **their arms.**

4

Chambered nautiluses can have as many as **90 tentacles.**

5

Because the **nautilus hasn't changed** much in **500 million years,** scientists often call it a **living fossil.**

6

The largest **giant squid** ever measured was almost 43 feet (13 m) long—that's **longer than a bus.**

7

Cuttlefish are **color-blind,** but they can **turn almost any color** to camouflage themselves.

Slippery Facts About Cephalopods

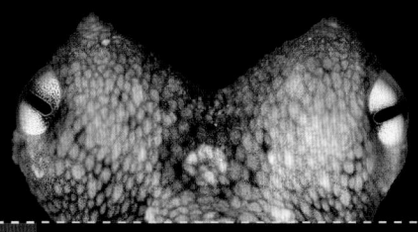

8

An **octopus** named Paul **correctly predicted** the winner of eight **World Cup soccer matches** in 2010.

9

The **gloomy octopus** is named for its **droopy, ghostly white eyes.**

10

The word **"cephalopod"**—a group of animals that includes **squid, octopuses, cuttlefish,** and **nautiluses**—means **"head-foot."**

Wild Facts About Parks and Preserves

1

Once the **private gardens** of five different Chinese dynasties and preserving more than **1,000 years of history,** Beihai Park in Beijing, China, was first opened for the public in 1925.

2

The world's **tallest waterfall,** Angel Falls in Venezuela's Canaima National Park is located **so deep in the forest** that visitors often choose to view it from the air.

3

With more than **400 miles** (644 km) **of caves,** Mammoth Cave National Park in Kentucky, U.S.A., protects **the longest** known **cave system** on Earth.

4

Virunga National Park, in the Democratic Republic of the Congo, safeguards **mountain gorillas,** endangered primates that can weigh **up to 400 pounds** (180 kg).

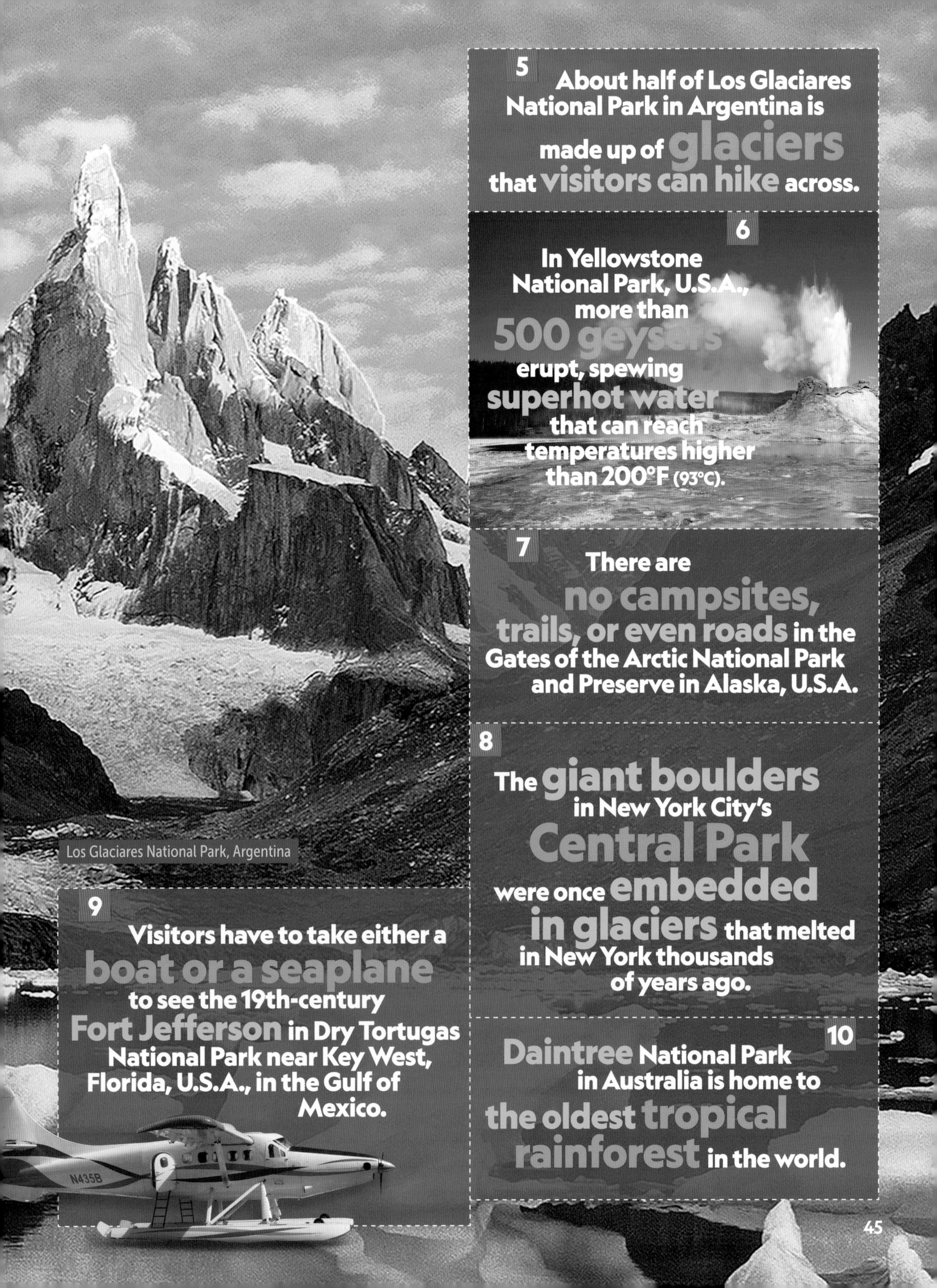

Los Glaciares National Park, Argentina

5 About half of Los Glaciares National Park in Argentina is made up of **glaciers** that **visitors can hike** across.

6 In Yellowstone National Park, U.S.A., more than **500 geysers** erupt, spewing **superhot water** that can reach temperatures higher than 200°F (93°C).

7 There are **no campsites, trails, or even roads** in the Gates of the Arctic National Park and Preserve in Alaska, U.S.A.

8 The **giant boulders** in New York City's **Central Park** were once **embedded in glaciers** that melted in New York thousands of years ago.

9 Visitors have to take either a **boat or a seaplane** to see the 19th-century **Fort Jefferson** in Dry Tortugas National Park near Key West, Florida, U.S.A., in the Gulf of Mexico.

10 **Daintree** National Park in Australia is home to **the oldest tropical rainforest** in the world.

1

After **millions of roses** are harvested in Qal'at Mgouna, Morocco, local residents take to the streets with decorated **floats** to celebrate the harvest.

2

To **celebrate winter,** marchers carrying torches at the Vulcan Victory Torchlight Parade **light up the darkness** in Saint Paul, Minnesota, U.S.A.

3

It takes **90 people** to fly the **largest balloons** at the Macy's Thanksgiving Day Parade in New York City.

4

Thousands of dancers from samba schools in Rio de Janeiro, Brazil, perform at the **Sambadrome** until dawn before judges and spectators during the **Rio Carnival.**

5

More than 70 different groups of revelers—or **"krewes"**—parade along the streets of New Orleans, Louisiana, U.S.A., during **Mardi Gras,** including the Rolling Elvi, people dressed like Elvis riding scooters.

6

Every inch of the floats in the annual **Rose Bowl Parade** in Pasadena, California, U.S.A., must be covered in either flowers or other **natural materials,** such as bark, seeds, or leaves.

7

In 1737, a **St. Patrick's Day parade** was held in Boston, Massachusetts, U.S.A.,—more than 160 years before Ireland held one to honor **its own patron saint.**

8

The Marksmen's Parade, in Hanover, Germany, started in the **15th century** as a showcase for people's **archery skills.**

9

In 1801, President **Thomas Jefferson** began the tradition of a **Fourth of July parade** outside the White House in Washington, D.C.

10

Every year, some **50 ships** aglow with **colored lights** parade through the harbor in Sydney, Australia, to **ring in the new year.**

Festive Facts About Parades

Sydney, Australia

Incredible Facts About Inventions

2

The first **functional submarine,** used during the American Revolution, was **made of wood** and named **the Turtle** because it looked like a **turtle shell.**

1

The **inventor** of the chocolate chip cookie sold her idea to Nestlé in exchange for a **lifetime supply** of **chocolate.**

3

Thomas **Edison's** laboratory was nicknamed the **Invention Factory.**

4

The temperature scale invented in 1742 by **Anders Celsius** was originally the opposite of the one we know today: 0 degrees was hot, and **100 degrees was cold.**

5

When he was a boy, **Benjamin Franklin** invented **paddles** for his hands to **help him swim faster.**

6

To ensure that no one tried to make the same product, **the inventor** of **pumpable hand soap** bought 100 million **small pumps** after his invention came out.

7

The **first model** of the **bicycle,** invented in 1817, didn't have any pedals.

8

The first **traffic signal** was invented in 1868 to direct **horse-drawn carriages,** not cars.

9

Italian artist **Leonardo da Vinci** invented a **scuba-like suit** for **underwater sneak attacks** on enemy ships.

10

The **can opener** was invented nearly **half a century** after the can was introduced.

Green Facts to Protect the Planet

1

Japanese scientists discovered a strain of bacteria at a recycling plant that **eats plastics.**

2

Recycling one million cell phones recovers about **75 pounds (34 kg) of gold.**

3

In Istanbul, Turkey, you get a **free subway ride** when you recycle a plastic bottle.

4

In one year, a mature tree absorbs 48 pounds (22 kg) of carbon dioxide from the atmosphere, which helps **clean the air.**

5

At a smoothie shop in Portland, Oregon, U.S.A., you can blend your own drink by pedaling a stationary bike attached to a blender.

6

Middle schoolers from New York, U.S.A., designed a device that fits on boats to filter out plastic from waterways.

Elephant poop powers some of the electricity at Munich Zoo in Germany.

7

In its lifetime, one reusable bag can replace 600 plastic bags.

8

9

Shutting off the water while you brush your teeth can save eight gallons (30 L) of water a day.

10

Old roof shingles are sometimes ground up and used to make new roads.

Deep Facts About Canyons

1

Daredevil Evel Knievel attempted to launch himself in a rocket over Snake River Canyon in Idaho, U.S.A., but he failed when his parachute opened too early. (He survived.)

2

A canyon in Death Valley National Park, which straddles California and Nevada, U.S.A., was nicknamed Star Wars Canyon because parts of the Star Wars movies were filmed there.

3

The pressure at the bottom of the Mariana Trench, an underwater canyon almost seven miles (11 km) down in the Pacific Ocean, is the equivalent of 50 jumbo jets piled on top of you.

4

The length of Valles Marineris, a canyon on Mars, is about the distance between the East Coast and the West Coast of the United States.

5

The Christmas Tree, a sparkling column covered in crystals, stands inside Slaughter Canyon Cave in Carlsbad Caverns National Park in New Mexico, U.S.A.

6

The **Andean condor,** found in Peru's Colca Canyon, has a **10-foot** (3-m) **wingspan.**

7

Tibet's Yarlung Tsangpo Grand Canyon is **three times deeper** than the **Grand Canyon.**

8

The **deepest land canyon** on Earth is **under the ice** in Antarctica.

9

While some canyons can take millions of years to form, **narrow slot canyons** are **created instantly** when flash floods hit soft rock.

10

Supai Village in Arizona's **Grand Canyon** is the only place in the United States where mail is still delivered by **pack mule.**

Grand Canyon National Park, U.S.A.

Extreme Weirdness

SUNBATHING POTATOES

WHAT Tater art

WHERE Berlin, Germany

DETAILS These aren't couch potatoes—they're beach potatoes! An artist fitted the veggies with tiny plastic sunglasses, then placed them under mini paper umbrellas on a beach-like patch of dirt. Talk about an a-peel-ing art project.

SCARY SNAKE CAKE

WHAT Reptile-shaped dessert

WHERE Kent, England

DETAILS This realistic-looking reptile is 100 percent cake. A baker created the Burmese python look-alike for her daughter's birthday party. Molding together cut-up portions of six separate cakes, it took the mom three days to create the final product. Next year's dessert might be a pie-thon.

REMOTE-CONTROLLED SUPERHERO

WHAT Superhero-shaped plane

WHERE San Diego, California, U.S.A.

DETAILS It's a bird! It's a plane! It's ... yup, it's a plane. The superhero-shaped flier—powered by a battery pack built into its "head" and operated with a remote control—took its first test flight over southern California. Made mostly of Styrofoam, the plane is just one of more than 30 pop-culture-themed fliers built by its creator. Guess you could say this is a highly cape-able aircraft.

PADDLING ON SAND

WHAT Dry river race

WHERE Alice Springs, Australia

DETAILS Sand ahoy! Regattas, or boat races, usually involve water. Not the annual Henley-on-Todd event. Contestants propel themselves with shovels from atop wheeled boogie boards, or run in groups carrying bathtubs over a dry riverbed. That's one way to make bath time more fun.

THE HANDS GO MARCHING IN

WHAT Carnaval parade

WHERE Ovar, Portugal

DETAILS Need a hand? Here are a few! Costumed paraders march down streets to celebrate Carnaval, a festival that lets people express their wild side after a couple months of winter. People often meet and walk around in kooky outfits, called masquerading, during Carnaval, which lasts about a week.

TRANSFORMER INVADES CITY

WHAT Transformer statue

WHERE London, England

DETAILS To promote the DVD release of *Transformers: Revenge of the Fallen*, a movie studio transformed the city's iconic "bendy buses" into, well, a Transformer. (A bendy bus is basically two buses attached so they can bend in the middle.) Towering 13 feet (4 m) tall, the Transformer was constructed out of real bus parts.

Massive Facts About Mega

1 In the 1930s, New York City became the world's first metropolitan area to have more than 10 million people.

2 Pizzerias in São Paulo, Brazil, make more than one million pizzas a day.

3 If you added up all the floor space in the shopping malls in Jakarta, the capital of Indonesia, it would cover more than 1,000 American football fields.

Shanghai, China

4 Located less than 10 miles (16 km) from downtown Cairo, Egypt, the Great Pyramid towers 481 feet (147 m) aboveground.

5 More people live in Shanghai, China, than in all of Chile.

Cities

6

The **ancient capital** of the Aztec, Tenochtitlan, is now the **center of Mexico City.**

7

The Shard, a skyscraper in London, England, is referred to as a **vertical city:** It has restaurants, apartments, and offices so residents never have to leave.

8

During peak hours, **thousands of people** pass through the **five crosswalks** of **Shibuya Crossing** in Tokyo, Japan.

9

Trains in Mumbai, India, were built to carry about **1,700 passengers,** but peak hours bring nearly **three times** that number.

10

In 2018, **33 metropolitan areas** across the world had more than **10 million people—** by 2030 it's estimated there will be **43.**

Facts Crawling With Bugs

1

The **Darth Vader** beetle is named for its dark, **helmetlike head.**

2

One species of wasp **lays an egg inside** a **ladybug.** The hatched larva **paralyzes** the ladybug, using it for food and protection.

3

Some moths **have ears** on **their mouths.**

4

A cockroach **can live** for weeks **without its head.**

5

Antarctic midge larvae spend more than **half of their life frozen.**

6

The scientific name for one species of **fairy fly** is ***Tinkerbella nana,*** after characters in ***Peter Pan.***

7

Houseflies **eat** their **own vomit.**

8

Fruit flies were the **first animals launched into space.**

Turn the page for more creepy-crawly facts!

9

Mosquitoes are attracted to **smelly feet.**

10

The **Pacific beetle cockroach** produces a **pale yellow "milk"** that is **more nutritious** than any other kind of milk.

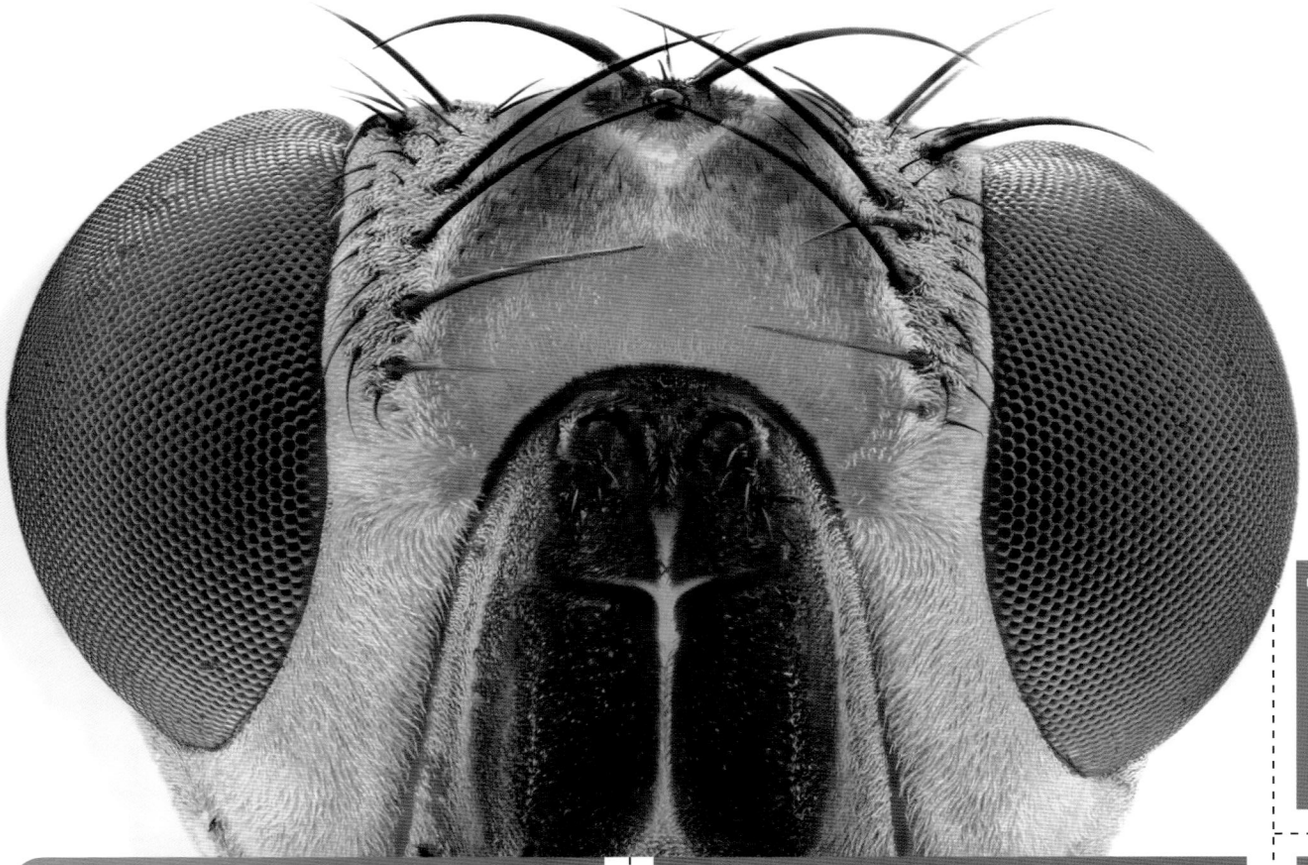

11

Insect blood is yellow, green, or **clear.**

12

One species of assassin bug carries the **dead bodies** of its prey, such as ants and termites, on its backs to **confuse predators.**

13

Scientists placed tiny solar-powered **backpacks on dragonflies** to see if the bugs could be used as drones to aid in **search and rescue missions.**

14

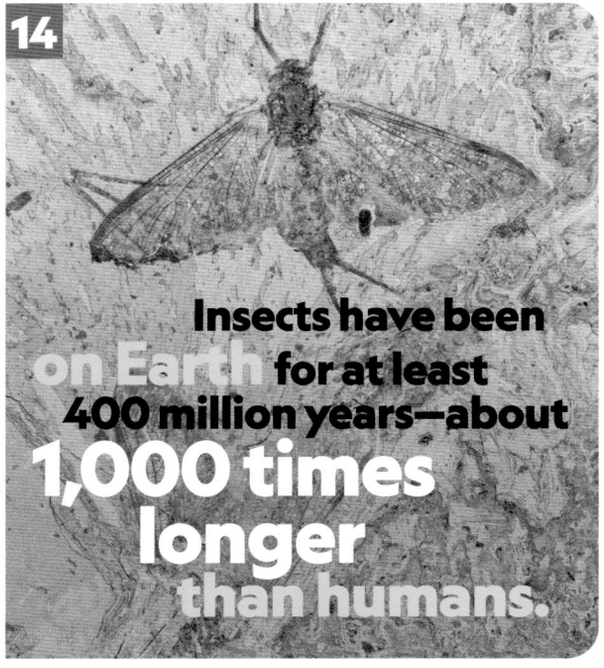

Insects have been **on Earth** for at least 400 million years—about **1,000 times longer than humans.**

15

Termites use **their own poop** to build their nests.

16

Insect poop is called **frass.**

17

Question Mark, Small Skipper, Red Admiral, and Painted Lady are names of types of **butterflies.**

18

Caterpillars have **12 eyes.**

19

Diving beetles can live underwater by breathing from an air bubble stored beneath their wings.

20

Most **beetles can't hear.**

Un-baa-lievable Facts About Barnyard

1 Ducks are social— they like to hang out in big groups with other ducks.

2 Chicken moms try to keep their chicks away from foods that aren't safe for them to eat.

3 Pigs wag their tails when frustrated.

4 Alpacas spit at one another when angry.

5 Cows chew their food for about eight hours a day.

Animals

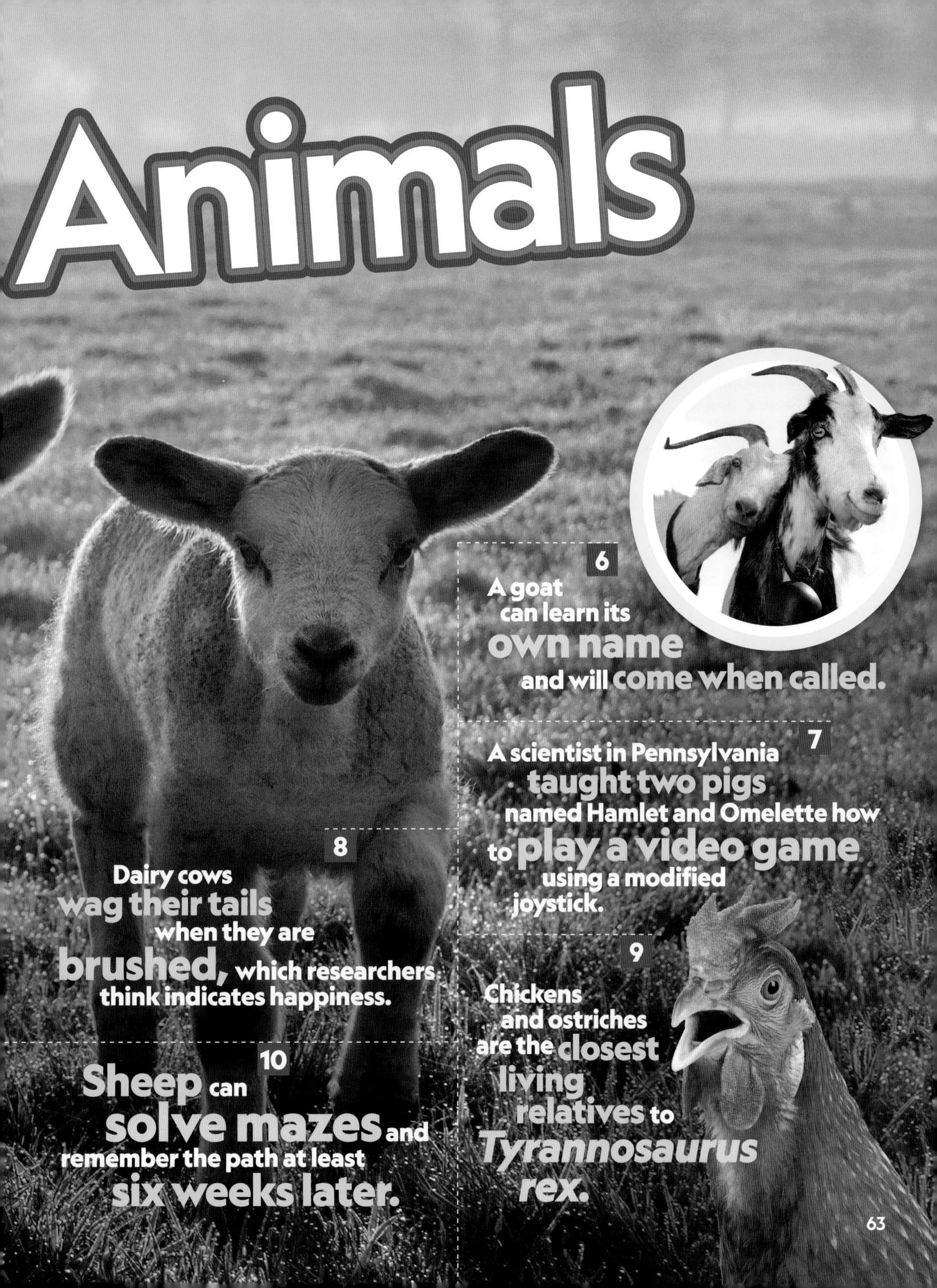

6

A goat can learn its **own name** and will **come when called.**

7

A scientist in Pennsylvania **taught two pigs** named Hamlet and Omelette how to **play a video game** using a modified joystick.

8

Dairy cows **wag their tails** when they are **brushed,** which researchers think indicates happiness.

9

Chickens and ostriches are the **closest living relatives** to ***Tyrannosaurus rex.***

10

Sheep can **solve mazes** and remember the path at least **six weeks later.**

Facts to Calculate About Computer History

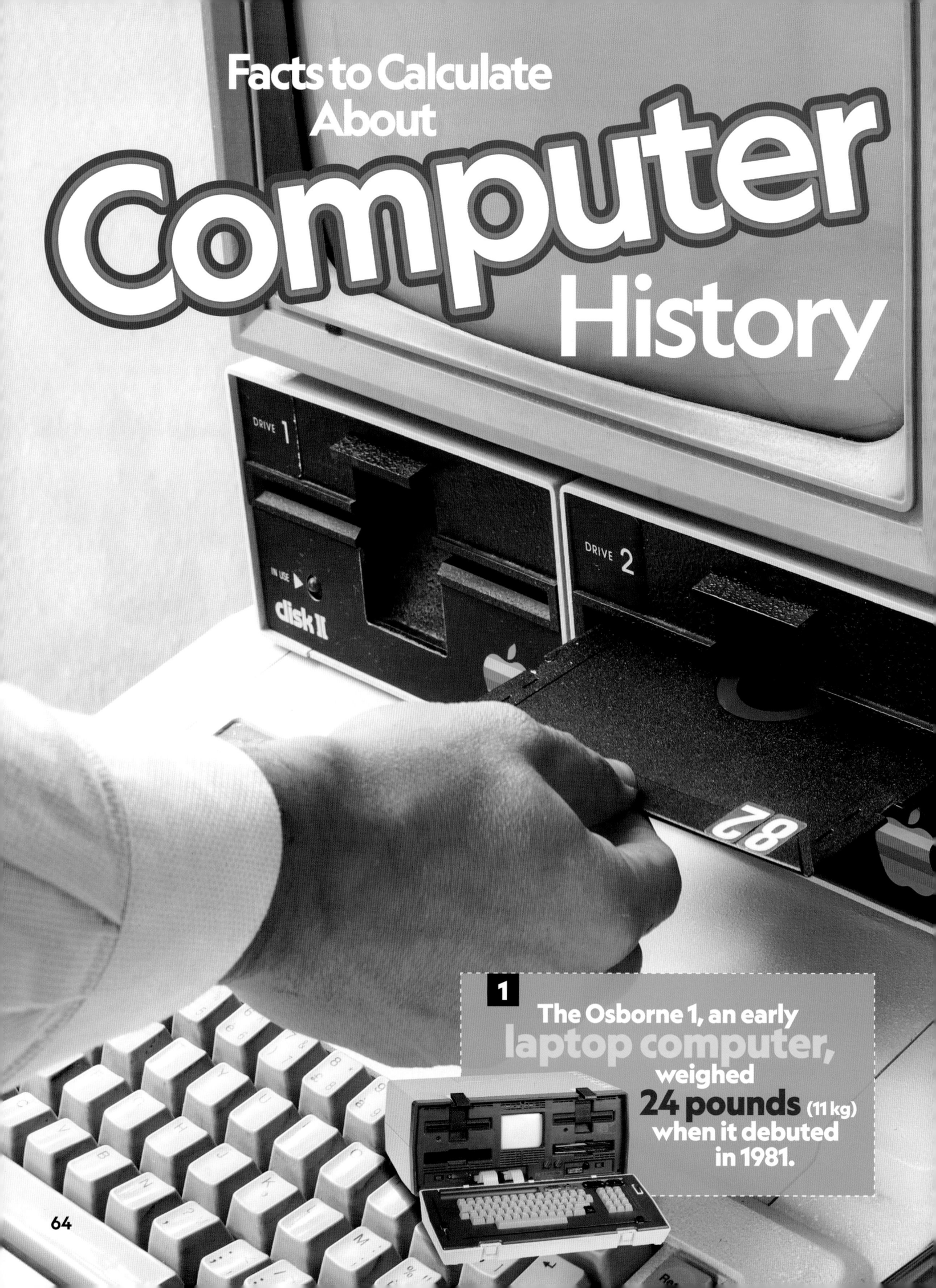

1

The Osborne 1, an early **laptop computer,** weighed **24 pounds** (11 kg) when it debuted in 1981.

2

In 2015, researchers at the University of Michigan in the United States created the **Micro Mote,** a computer so small that nearly **150** could fit into a thimble.

3

President **Bill Clinton** became the first American president to **send an email—** a message **to astronaut John Glenn** while he was on the space shuttle.

4

In **the 1960s,** J. C. R. Licklider, a scientist at the Massachusetts Institute of Technology, had an idea for a **global network** of computers he called the **Galactic Network.**

5

In the late 1800s, **looms were programmed** to read **punched cards** that contained instructions on how to make cloth.

6

In the 1820s, English mathematician **Charles Babbage** imagined a type of **calculator** powered by a steam engine—when built, it had **8,000 parts** and was eight feet (2.4 m) tall.

7

In 1946, in a **science fiction** short story called "A Logic Named Joe," the world was connected by a **network of computers.**

8

On October 29, 1969, the internet's **first message** was sent between two computers at two California universities—**the message was "lo,"** as the system **crashed** before the full word **"login"** could be sent.

9

Nicknamed the **"fuzzball,"** an early **internet router** developed in the 1970s could send **300 packets** of information a second. (Routers today can handle more than one billion a second.)

10

Tim Berners-Lee, the inventor of the **World Wide Web,** was **knighted** by Queen Elizabeth II.

Freewheeling Facts About Bicycles

1

Considered by many as the birthplace of **bikepacking,** the nearly 3,000-mile (4,828-km)-long **Great Divide Mountain Bike Route** follows the Rocky Mountains from Jasper, Alberta, Canada, to Antelope Wells, New Mexico, U.S.A.

2

A man in Lithuania created a **3,053-pound** (1,385-kg) **rideable bicycle—** the **heaviest** in the world.

3

Before they built airplanes, **Orville and Wilbur Wright sold bikes** they made in their Dayton, Ohio, U.S.A., shop.

4

The **leader** of the **Tour de France** wears a **yellow jersey** because the newspaper that first sponsored the race was printed on yellow paper.

5

Nicknamed **boneshakers,** bikes made of iron and wood gave people a **very bumpy** ride in the 1860s.

6

Bicycle motocross (BMX), a sport in which riders **race bicycles around a track,** became an Olympic sport in the 2008 Summer Games.

7

Karl von Drais, an **early bicyclemaker,** realized that people **could balance** while moving forward on two wheels by **watching ice skaters.**

8

At the Indy Crit Bicycle Parade in Indianapolis, Indiana, U.S.A., you can watch **brass and polka bands** play while they ride, as well as bicyclists on **"costumed" bikes.**

9

Astronauts on the **International Space Station** can still **ride a bike—** it's known as the Cycle Ergometer with Vibration Isolation and Stabilization System (CEVIS).

10

In 2016, people in the Netherlands traveled more than **9.6 billion miles** (15.5 billion km) by bike—that's more than **20,200 trips to the moon** and back!

Facts About Breakfast Foods to Wake You Up

1

Canada has more doughnut shops per person than any other country.

2

Competitors at a pancake race in Olney, England, wear an apron and run holding a frying pan containing a hot pancake.

3

More than half of Americans eat cereal for breakfast, a survey found.

4

The word **"bagel"** comes from a German word meaning **"bracelet."**

5

Coffee beans aren't beans—they're **seeds.**

6

The cofounder of Nike used a **waffle iron** to make the company's first pair of **Waffle Trainer** running shoes.

7

It takes **40 gallons** (151 L) of **maple tree sap** to make one gallon (3.8 L) of **maple syrup.**

8

The **largest pancake** ever made was **49 feet** (15 m) wide.

9

If an egg **spins easily** on a flat surface, **it's cooked,** but if it **wobbles, it's raw.**

10

It takes about **three oranges** to make **one glass** of orange juice.

Extraordinary Facts About the Future

1

Fashion designers are looking to design **clothes that "grow"** as kids grow, using **stretchy material** and pleats that **unfold.**

2

To reduce **pollution** and the cost of **transporting food,** cities may soon have **floating farms** in nearby bodies of water.

3

Drones may soon replace drivers for **delivering** everything from packages to **pizza.**

4

Plans are underway for people to travel through **underground tubes** in pods that cruise **faster than a jet.**

5

Plastic may soon be made from **biodegradable** materials such as **algae or fish skin.**

6

Future astronauts on their journey to Mars may grow **algae-based food** that tastes like **caviar.**

7

"Smart" contact lenses will not only correct vision but will also **display** information like **directions** and **sports scores.**

8

Instead of **fitness bracelets,** people may soon wear clothing made with **"smart fabric"** that measures heart rates.

9

Boeing has plans to make a **hypersonic airplane** that can fly from **New York City** to **London** in two hours. (It currently takes seven hours.)

10

Instead of a physician or nurse, **robots** will **take your temperature** and **blood pressure** at the doctor's office.

What's the Difference?

Check out these similar pairings and see how you can determine this from that!

PORCUPINE VS. HEDGEHOG

Porcupines and hedgehogs are not closely related, but their pokey form of protection makes them equally eye-catching. Porcupines are about three feet (1 m) long (not including the tail), and they live on every continent except Australia and Antarctica. These herbivores spend much of their time in trees eating fruits and plants. They have as many as 30,000 quills, which typically lay flat on their backs, but when the animal is threatened, they stand straight up. The quills detach easily and are painful to the predator that gets poked! Hedgehogs are only five to 12 inches (13 to 31 cm) long and spend their time in hedges and under logs, looking for insects, worms, snails, and frogs to eat. They aren't quite as widespread as porcupines: They live in the wild in Europe, Asia, Africa, and New Zealand. Hedgehogs have stiff, sharp spines that they use as protection. When threatened, hedgehogs roll up into a spiky ball to protect their soft bellies. Hedgehog spines don't easily detach.

Hedgehog

VEIN VS. ARTERY

Arteries carry blood away from the heart, and veins carry it back again. But it's not that simple. There are two types of circulation in your body: systemic circulation—blood travels all around your body—and pulmonary circulation—blood travels from the heart to the lungs and back to the heart again. ("Pulmonary" just means something related to the lungs.) The pulmonary artery carries blood away from the heart to the lungs so the blood can become rich in oxygen, and then pulmonary veins bring the oxygen-rich blood to the heart, which pumps it around the body. Then super-small branches of blood vessels called capillaries link arteries and veins. That's when the veins take over, carrying the blood back to the heart, where the cycle starts all over again.

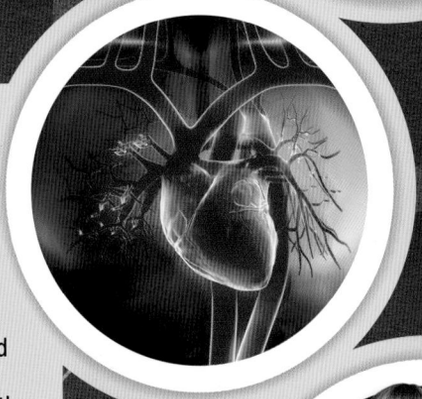

NECTAR VS. POLLEN

Have you heard the expression "busy as a bee"? Why are bees so busy? The answer has to do with nectar and pollen. Bees visit flowers and slurp up plant nectar, a sugary liquid. The nectar is held in a special "honey" stomach to take back to the hive. There, bees pass the nectar from mouth to mouth in a process that turns it into honey. When bees visit flowers, they also brush up against pollen grains, which stick to their bodies. Some of this pollen falls off when they fly to other plants, which is how the plants reproduce. As for humans, pollen might make us sneeze, but honey makes us happy!

FIELD HOCKEY VS. LACROSSE

Lacrosse and field hockey are both played on a field with players using sticks to pass a small ball. But that's where the similarities end between these two sports, which have been played in various parts of the world for centuries. Field hockey has 11 players on each team who move the ball on the ground using a stick rounded at the end. The goal is to pass and shoot the ball into the opponent's goal. Think of it as soccer, but you use a stick instead of your feet. In lacrosse, a team of 10 players throws and catches the ball in the air with sticks that have a net on the end. Lacrosse is more of a contact sport than field hockey, and players wear more protective gear, including pads and face masks. Lacrosse does have the same objective as field hockey: Score more goals than the other team.

Lacrosse

ROBOT VS. ANDROID

Here's the difference between a robot and an android: An android is a robot, but a robot isn't necessarily an android. Confused? Let's break it down. A robot is a machine that can carry out tasks written into a computer program. Even though it can execute a task on its own, a human has to program what it does. For example, the self-cleaning robots that zip around the living room sweeping up pet hair are robots. Androids are robots and are programmed just like other robots, but they look like humans. This is the stuff of science fiction that's becoming reality. In Japan, an android named Erica works as a newscaster. She looks like a person and even talks and moves like her human counterpart. While robots and androids seem futuristic, similar ideas have been around for a long time. In 1495, Italian artist and inventor Leonardo da Vinci created an armored suit that moved with the help of pulleys, cables, gears, and wheels. It could even wave its sword and open and close its mouth!

Android

GLACIER VS. ICEBERG

Glaciers and icebergs are both made of ice, but if you had to spend the night on one, a glacier is the safer bet! That's because icebergs form when parts of a glacier break off and start to float in the ocean or a lake. This is known as calving. Glaciers form in areas where masses of snow turn into ice over time, so they are always on land. If you were on an iceberg, you'd travel along with the water currents. Since the chunks that break off glaciers come in all different sizes, scientists use the word "icebergs" to refer to pieces at least 16 feet (5 m) across.

1

Impalas, a type of antelope, can jump 10 feet (3 m) high—that's the height of an elephant.

2

A giraffe's eye is as big as a Ping-Pong ball.

3

A black rhino's horns grow three inches (8 cm) every year.

4

A zebra's skin is black under its striped coat.

5

As many as 1.5 million wildebeest migrate 620 miles (1,000 km) across Africa's Serengeti each year in search of food.

Surprising Facts About Animals on the Serengeti

6 A dik-dik, the smallest Serengeti antelope, is the size of a miniature poodle.

7 Leopards get most of the water they need from eating their prey.

8 A lion's heels don't touch the ground when it walks.

9 Scientists can tell how old a hyena is and where it ranks in its clan based on the sound of its "laugh."

10 With their strong jaws, hippos can snap a canoe in half with one bite.

1

Crocodiles survived the extinction event that **killed the dinosaurs.**

2

A **brown bear** is an apex predator that weighs as much as 800 pounds (363 kg), but much of its diet consists of nuts, berries, leaves, and roots.

3

About as big as a dinner plate, the Goliath birdeater is large enough to **eat birds,** but it usually eats mice, frogs, and lizards.

4

Snow leopards can leap as far as 50 feet (15 m), taking down prey three times their own weight.

5

The **tongue** of a blue whale, which helps it swallow millions of shrimplike animals called krill each day, can weigh as much as an elephant.

6

A single gray wolf can eat **20 pounds** (9 kg) **of meat** in one sitting—that's like you eating 80 hamburgers.

7

After a chase, a cheetah needs a half hour to **catch its breath** before it can eat.

8

The **black king snake** is resistant to the toxins of venomous snakes and often preys on rattlesnakes, copperheads, and cottonmouths.

9

Frigate birds hunt over the ocean but will drown if they get wet, so they have to **catch flying fish** or steal fish caught by other seabirds.

10

At only about three pounds (1.4 kg), the **fennec fox** is about the size of a kitten but has giant six-inch (15-cm) ears it uses to hear prey underneath the sand.

Powerful Predator Facts

1 Two **giant concrete hands** support a nearly 500-foot (152-m)-tall **walking bridge** outside Da Nang, Vietnam.

2 **Giant tree roots** have grown into the 12th-century Ta Prohm Temple, a former monastery in Angkor Wat, Cambodia, **merging buildings** and **forest.**

3 It took about **20,000 workers** to build India's **Taj Mahal** in the 1600s.

4 Paddlers **race boats** fashioned with **dragon heads** and tails in Hong Kong's annual Dragon Boat Festival.

5 When building China's **Great Wall,** workers added **sticky rice** to the mortar to increase its strength.

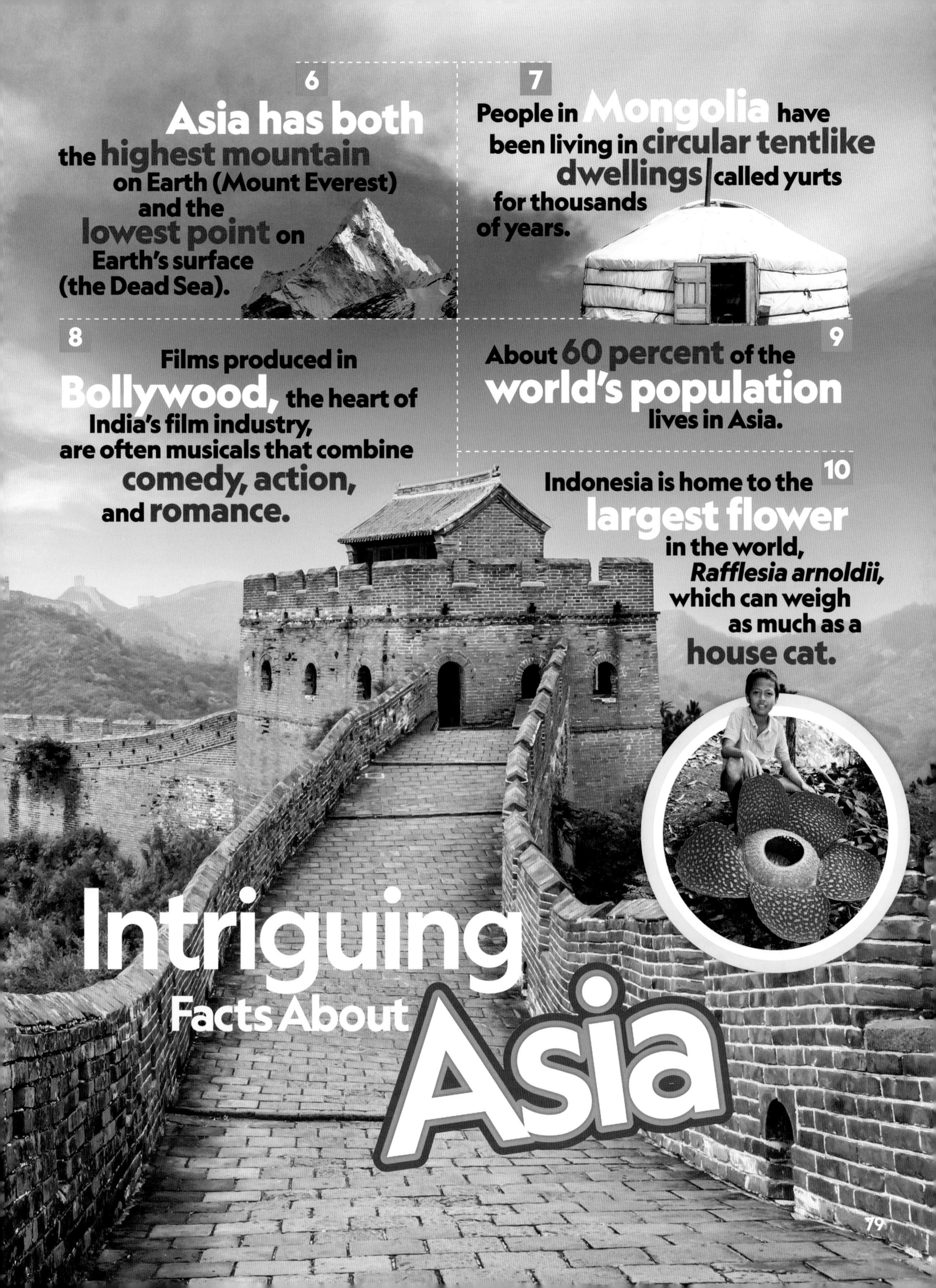
6
Asia has both the highest mountain on Earth (Mount Everest) and the lowest point on Earth's surface (the Dead Sea).
7
People in Mongolia have been living in circular tentlike dwellings called yurts for thousands of years.
8
Films produced in Bollywood, the heart of India's film industry, are often musicals that combine comedy, action, and romance.
9
About 60 percent of the world's population lives in Asia.
10
Indonesia is home to the largest flower in the world, Rafflesia arnoldii, which can weigh as much as a house cat.
Intriguing Facts About Asia

Open These Facts About Shells

1

The **whooshing sound** you hear when you put a **seashell to your ear** isn't the ocean; it's the shell making the **noises around you** louder.

2

Scientists found **carvings on shells** that *Homo erectus*, **an ancestor** of modern humans, **may have made** half a million years ago.

3

Most seashells are **right-handed**—they open to the right.

4

Oysters grow on each other, creating reefs that form a **community** for many types of marine animals.

3,000 years ago in Peru, people used seashells as **musical instruments.**

6

5 When some hermit crabs **smell a dead hermit crab,** they scurry to the site to **eat the carcass—** and one might even **move into the shell.**

Most seashells are the **outer skeletons** of animals known as **mollusks.**

8

7

When a seashell **has a hole in it,** that usually means a **predator drilled** into it to eat the animal inside.

9

Thousands of years ago in China and Africa, seashells were **used as money.**

10

Female argonaut octopuses **build delicate, paperlike shells** to lay their eggs in.

1

There are nearly **600 species** of carnivorous plants, and they can be found on **every continent** except Antarctica.

2

Bladderworts, which **trap prey** in **bladder-shaped sacs,** can snap up mosquito larvae **faster than a blink** of an eye.

3

After a fire, some carnivorous plants can **grow back** within days.

4

Large **pitcher plants** can hold **two gallons** (7.6 L) of liquid.

5

Carnivorous plants **secrete digestive juices** in the same way a **human stomach** does.

Meaty Facts About Carnivorous Plants

6

A sundew plant in Australia uses **sticky tentacles** to **capture insects.**

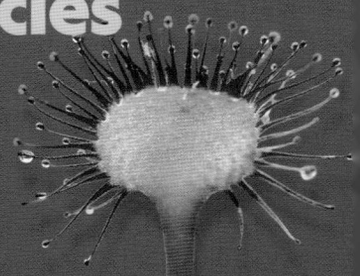

7

Venus flytraps **digest ants and spiders,** but they **don't consume bees,** which pollinate them.

8

Small rats and tree shrews on the island of Borneo **slurp nectar** from the lids of **pitcher plants** and then "feed" the plant by **pooping into its pitcher.**

9

Most pitcher plants have two kinds of pitchers—ones low to the ground to catch **crawling insects** and ones higher up to catch **flying ones.**

10

Researchers found that pitcher plants in Canada's Algonquin Provincial Park **digest small salamanders**—the first time a North American carnivorous plant was found to **snack on amphibians.**

Venus flytrap

1

When on the ground, sloths move by digging their front claws into the ground and dragging themselves along.

2

Sloths must come down out of the trees—and risk being eaten by a predator—to poop on the ground.

3

The three-toed sloth—the slowest moving mammal on Earth—is so still that predators like the harpy eagle have trouble spotting it.

4

A sloth spends almost its entire life hanging upside down.

5

The two-toed sloth has three toes on its back legs (but two fingers on its front ones).

6

About 10,000 years ago, a sloth as big as an elephant lived in what is now South America.

7

A sloth can turn its head almost all the way around.

8

Sloths poop about once a week.

9

The fur of a three-toed sloth is full of insects, and birds like the brown jay swoop down to eat the bugs from it.

10

Sloths are excellent swimmers and can hold their breath underwater for up to 40 minutes.

Sloth Facts to Hang Out With

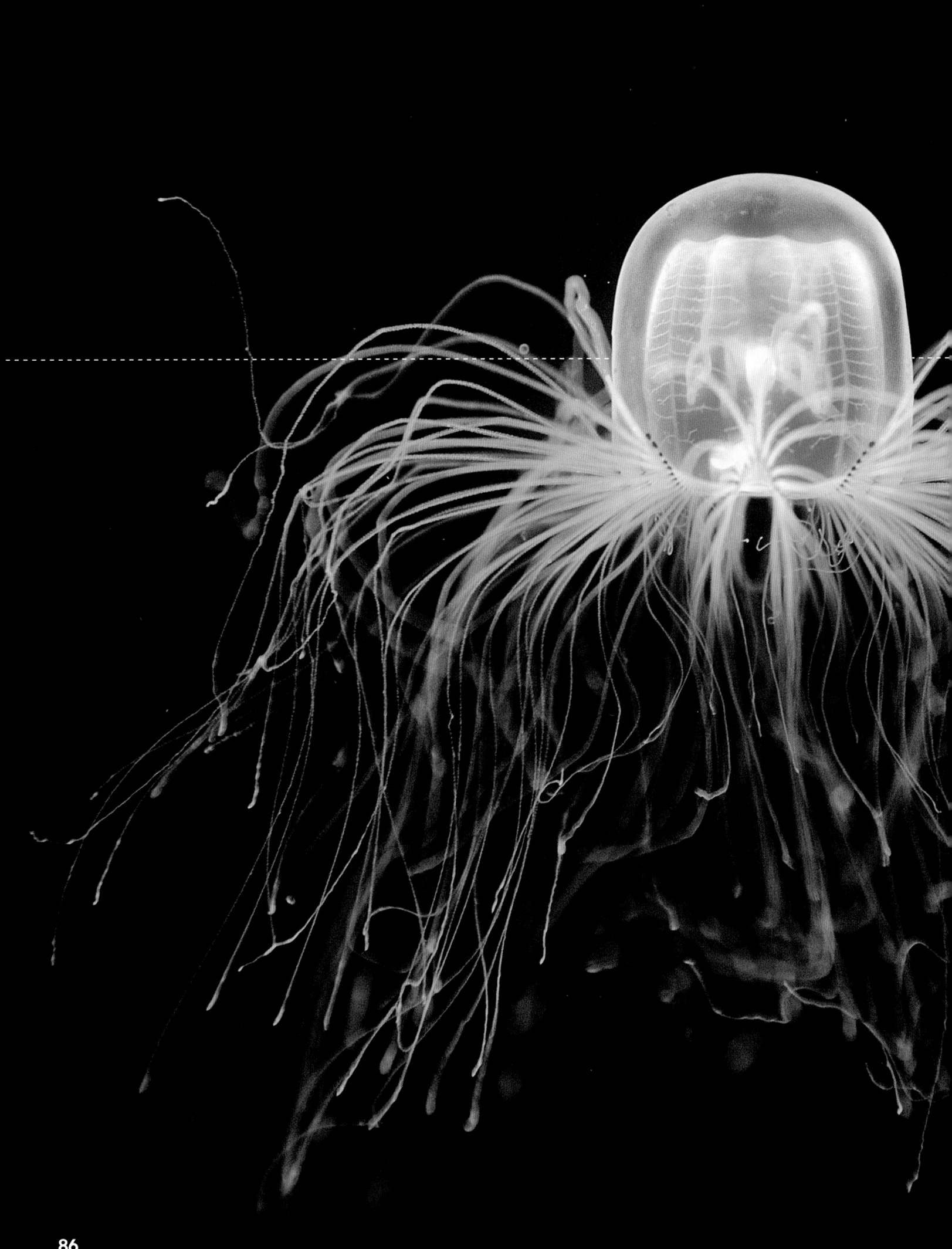

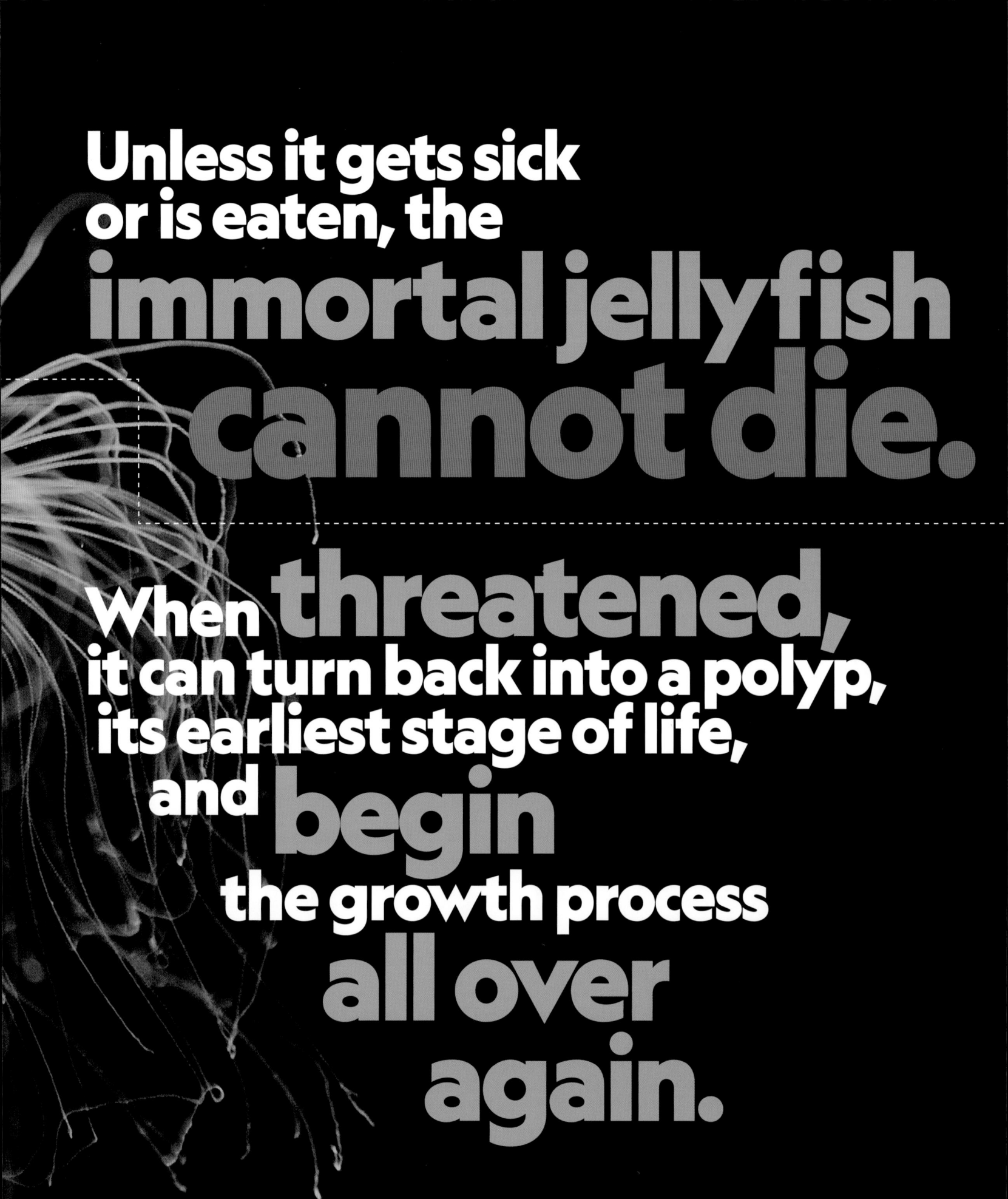
Unless it gets sick
or is eaten, the
immortal jellyfish
cannot die.
When threatened,
it can turn back into a polyp,
its earliest stage of life,
and begin
the growth process
all over
again.

1 The Baikal seal, found only in Siberia's Lake Baikal, has big, bulging eyes to help it find prey in the world's deepest lake.

2 Almost 70 percent of Earth's freshwater is found in ice caps and glaciers.

3 The Nile River—the world's longest river—originates in streams in East Africa and flows more than 4,000 miles (6,400 km) northward before emptying into the Mediterranean Sea.

Splashy Facts About Rivers and Lakes

Melissani Lake

4

Every day, some **100 million gallons** (379 million L) of water flow from the spring at **Manatee Springs** State Park, in Florida, U.S.A., into the Suwannee River.

5

NASA scientists calculated that **the amount of water** in the reservoir of the **Three Gorges Dam** on China's Yangtze River **lengthened** a day on Earth by .06 microseconds.

6

You can see **262 feet** (80 m) into New Zealand's **Blue Lake**, which is why it's known as the **clearest lake** in the world.

7

In 2007, it took Martin Strel **66 days to swim** the full length of the **Amazon River** in South America.

8

At 12,500 feet (3,810 m) in elevation, **Lake Titicaca** in South America is the **world's highest lake** that large boats can navigate.

9

The European country of **Finland** has nearly **188,000 lakes.**

10

In 1953, an **earthquake** on the Greek island of Kefalonia caused **rocks to collapse, revealing a lake** in Melissani Cave.

Elemental Facts About Elements

1

Earth's core is a **white-hot solid ball** made mostly of **iron.**

2

Helium balloons float because helium is **lighter than air.**

3

The **periodic table of elements** has been used to **predict the existence** of elements before they were discovered.

Europium, which **glows red** under ultraviolet light, is used in European paper money to help **prevent forgery.**

6

4

Every living thing on Earth contains **carbon.**

5

Ancient Romans **paid their soldiers** in sodium chloride, also known as **table salt.**

7

Helium was used in the **first rockets** that carried astronauts into space and in the **lunar lander** that put the first humans **on the moon.**

8

Russian scientist Dmitri Mendeleev created the **periodic table of elements,** which he claimed he saw in a **dream.**

9

Sodium explodes if you toss it into **water.**

10

Scientists are looking to **the Arctic, the deep sea, asteroids,** and **the moon** to **mine for elements.**

1

More than three million lights, which change patterns every minute, illuminate a floating 278-foot (85-m)-tall metal tree in the Rodrigo de Freitas Lagoon in Rio de Janeiro, Brazil.

2

During the summer solstice in Latvia, people raise poles topped with burning barrels to symbolize the victory of light over darkness.

3

In 1880, American inventor Thomas Edison created the first strand of electric lights.

4

In 2015, a 56-foot (17-m)-tall giant holiday ball was strung with 23,120 lights in Moscow, Russia.

5

Some holiday lights can be seen from outer space.

6

Since 1951, the lighting of the Christmas tree at Rockefeller Center in New York City has been broadcast live all over the world.

Holiday

Facts to Light Up Your Day

7

The 30-foot (9-m)-high **National Menorah** in Washington, D.C., is lit from a **cherry picker.**

8

In 1903, when people could first buy **strings of Christmas lights,** they had to **hire an electrician** to set them up.

9

During **Diwali,** the festival of lights, people in the town of Ayodhya, India, lit more than **900,000 oil lamps**—a world record.

10

At a winter **light festival** in Kanagawa, Japan, the **hills are covered** with some six million **LED lights.**

Could a new discovery help solve this ancient puzzle?

Dazzling rays from the sun burst through a strange ring of stones set on a grassy field. Some of these rocks rise 20 feet (6 m) in the air. Others lie scattered on the ground. This huge monument, called Stonehenge, has towered above England's Salisbury Plain for thousands of years—but it's still one of the world's biggest mysteries.

THE UNEXPLAINED

For centuries people have tried to unlock Stonehenge's secrets. A legend from the 12th century claimed that giants placed the monument on a mountain in Ireland, then a wizard named Merlin magically moved the stone circle to England. Other theories have suggested that migrants from continental Europe built the site as an astronomical observatory or as a temple to the sun and moon gods. No theories have been proved. But a new find may provide more information about the builders of Stonehenge and could help explain why the monument was constructed in this region.

HUNTING FOR CLUES

Many scientists had guessed that the builders of Stonehenge were the first to settle the area some 5,000 years ago, around 3000 B.C., when construction on the site began. A recent excavation is making people rethink this idea. While digging around a spring about a mile and a half (2.4 km) from Stonehenge, archaeologist David Jacques and his team uncovered hundreds of bones belonging to aurochs—a species of cattle twice the size of a modern-day bull that thrived in ancient times. In fact the site, known as Vespasian's Camp, held the largest collection of auroch bones ever found in Europe. That suggests that the spring was a pit stop along an auroch migration route where the animals drank water. The team also unearthed 31,000 flints, a stone tool used for hunting. "We started to wonder if the area was also a hunting ground and feasting site for ancient people," Jacques says. "Just one auroch could've fed a hundred people, so the place would've been a big draw." One of the excavated flints was made from a type of rock found some 75 miles (121 km) to the west. "This means people may have traveled from all over to hunt here," Jacques says. The animal bones and tools date back to 7500 B.C. The age of the artifacts caused Jacques to conclude that people moved to the region around 9,500 years ago—4,500 years earlier than what some had thought—to hunt auroch. And he thinks descendants of these settlers assembled the mysterious stone ring.

STONEHENGE, THE PREQUEL?

The first settlers may have even had their own early version of Stonehenge. Jacques thinks they set up a group of wooden posts 650 feet from where Stonehenge now stands. At least 8,500 years old, the posts were found during construction of a parking lot. This wooden monument may have been a tribute to the settlers' ancestors. Jacques and other scientists will keep digging for more clues that just might solve the mysteries of Stonehenge once and for all. But for now its story isn't written in stone.

STONE ZONE

It's too bad a wizard didn't help build Stonehenge. It was made with 4,000-pound bluestone rocks, and 50,000-pound sarsen stones. Funded in part by the National Geographic Society, archaeologist Mike Parker Pearson is studying where the stones originated and how people moved them to their current spot without wheeled vehicles. The sarsens were possibly hauled in on big wooden sleds from 20 miles away. The bluestones were traced to rock outcrops 140 miles away in present-day Wales, in the United Kingdom. Parker Pearson thinks they could have been dragged on sleds to a waterway and then floated on rafts to the building site. Parker Pearson is also investigating if the bluestones were first set up as circular monuments in Wales, then dismantled and taken to Salisbury Plain. One thing's for sure: The builders must've had rock-hard muscles.

An illustration of the massive auroch

The Secrets of Stonehenge

Brilliant Facts About the Color Blue

1

Only about **8 to 10 percent** of people have **blue eyes.**

2

Dust in Earth's atmosphere can **make the moon look blue.**

3

A **"blue moon"** doesn't mean the moon is blue—it's the **second full moon** to appear in a **single month.**

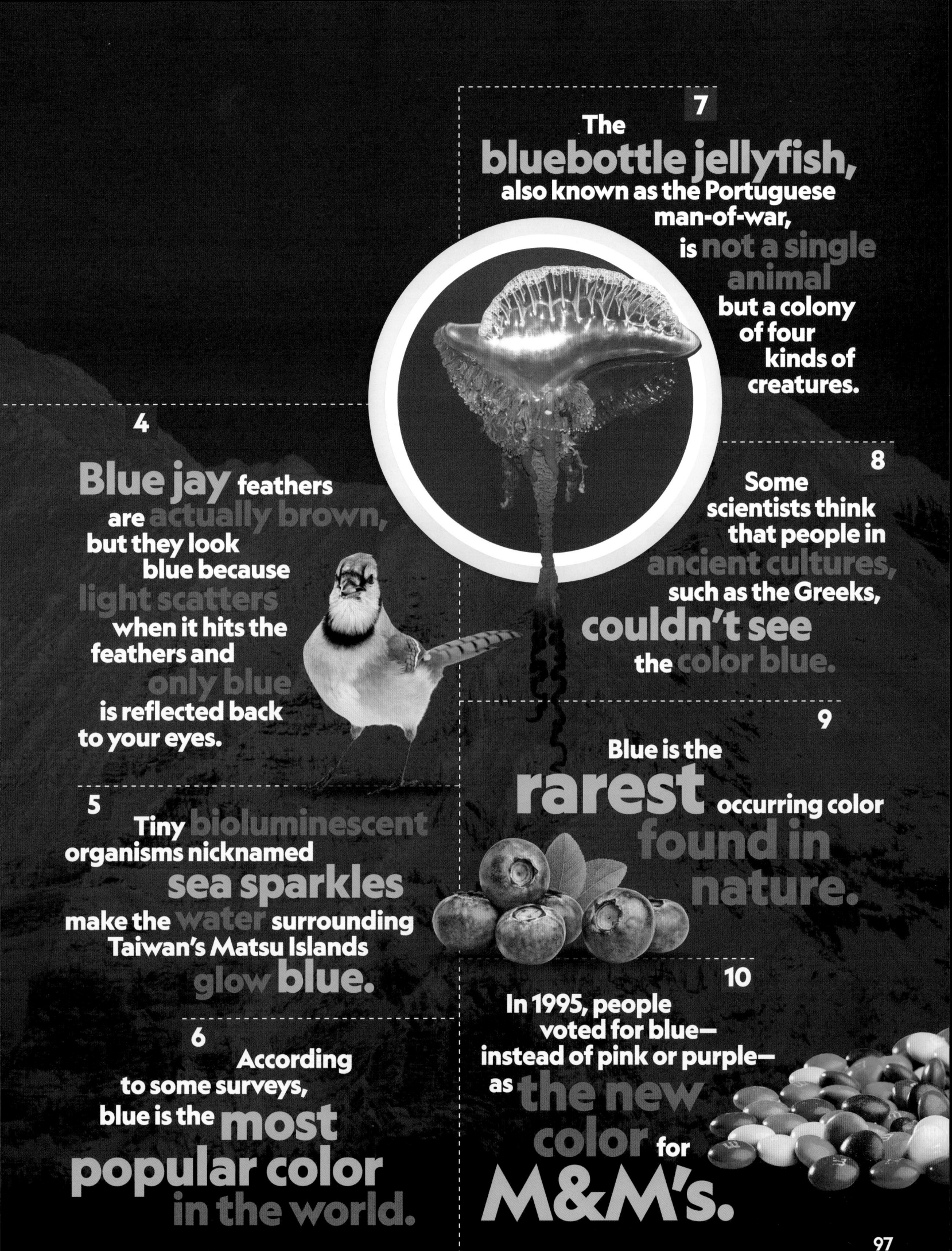

7

The **bluebottle jellyfish,** also known as the Portuguese man-of-war, is **not a single animal** but a colony of four kinds of creatures.

4

Blue jay feathers are **actually brown,** but they look blue because **light scatters** when it hits the feathers and **only blue** is reflected back to your eyes.

8

Some scientists think that people in **ancient cultures,** such as the Greeks, **couldn't see** the **color blue.**

5

Tiny **bioluminescent** organisms nicknamed **sea sparkles** make the **water** surrounding Taiwan's Matsu Islands **glow blue.**

9

Blue is the **rarest** occurring color **found in nature.**

6

According to some surveys, blue is the **most popular color in the world.**

10

In 1995, people voted for blue—instead of pink or purple—as **the new color** for **M&M's.**

Snack on Cookies

Tasty Facts About

1 In the United States, the **first week in December** is National **Cookie Cutter** Week.

2 In Asia, **Oreos** come in **green tea** flavor.

3 A bakery in North Carolina, U.S.A., once baked a **chocolate chip cookie** that was **102 feet** (31 m) across—that's about the length of **two semitrailers.**

4 In 2018, Nabisco redesigned its **animal crackers box** to show the animals **free in the wild** rather than in cages.

5

Fortune cookies were invented in Japan, not China.

6

Because of sugar, butter, and flour shortages during World War II, Girl Scouts sold calendars rather than cookies to raise money.

7

Cookie Monster's cookies are actually rice cakes painted to look like cookies.

8

A bakery in Cork, Ireland, once baked 4,695 cookies in one hour.

9

Boxes of animal crackers were originally intended as Christmas tree ornaments.

10

The first chocolate chip cookie was the size of a quarter.

Nighttime Facts About Nocturnal Animals

1

Barn owls are able to **swoop up prey** silently because the **soft edges** of their wings **muffle sound.**

2

Moonrats, a type of mammal, **mark their territory** at night with a scent that smells like **rotten garlic.**

3

A tarsier's **eyeball** is **bigger than** its **brain;** it uses its big peepers to see at night.

4

Whiskers on a **fox's legs** help it feel its way **through tall grass** at night.

7

The tube-lipped nectar bat, which feeds on flower nectar at night, has a tongue that's longer than its body.

5

To escape predators, an opossum sometimes plays "dead," flopping on its side with its tongue out.

8

Some scientists think a raccoon's "mask" marking helps reduce glare so it can see better at night.

6

Wolverines, which hunt at night, can smell hibernating prey buried 20 feet (6 m) under snow.

9

After sunset, an aardvark hunts and licks up some 50,000 ants with its sticky tongue.

10

Bush babies make a call that sounds like a human baby crying.

1

Dung beetles **eat poop** from mammals and can **carry a ball of dung** that's **50 times** their own weight.

2

Microscopic mites live in pores **on your face,** and they come out **when you're asleep.**

3

Wood rats pee all over **their nests,** which helps preserve them.

Funky Facts

That Will Gross You Out

4

Burrowing beetles **lay their eggs** near a **dead animal,** such as a mouse or a snake, so that the newly hatched baby beetles will have a **ready meal.**

5

Owls often **regurgitate** their prey's **teeth and bones** because they **can't digest** them.

6

Pacific hagfish **burrow inside** the body of a **dead animal** to eat it from the **inside out.**

7

The common eider, a kind of duck, **covers its eggs** in its **own droppings** when startled from its nest, which might keep predators away.

8

One species of beaded lacewing **stuns and kills** its prey **by tooting** on it.

9

A bombardier beetle shoots **toxins from its bottom** to protect itself.

10

The **tongue-eating louse slurps blood** from a fish's tongue until the tongue withers away, and then the louse becomes the **new "tongue"** in the fish's mouth.

1

Pirates rarely **buried treasure**— either because they **preferred to spend it** or because the loot was food or clothing.

2

An English merchant buried **six bags of silver** (he had bought the loot from pirates) in the York River in Virginia, U.S.A., but was **turned in** before he could **retrieve the riches.**

3

A 1692 earthquake and tsunami **nearly destroyed** the **pirate stronghold** of Port Royal, Jamaica— the **sea swallowed** about two-thirds of the city.

4

Madame Ching Shih, a powerful early-19th-century **Chinese pirate,** commanded some **80,000 men.** (Blackbeard commanded about 300.)

Pirate Facts That Will Shiver Your Timbers

5

Pirate pair **Rachel and George Wall** targeted ships off the New Hampshire, U.S.A., coast by pretending to need help.

6

Pirates in early America called their coins **"pieces of eight,"** which were Spanish silver dollar coins that often had an "8" stamped on them.

7

A **black flag** meant that pirates would spare the lives of sailors who surrendered, but a red flag signaled no mercy.

8

Legend holds that Blackbeard's **headless body** was buried on Ocracoke Island on the Outer Banks of North Carolina, U.S.A., after he was killed there in November 1718.

9

Pirates followed a **strict code of laws** on board—and rule breakers could be severely punished.

10

It's unlikely that pirates ever made people **walk the plank.**

Extreme Weirdness

ATTACK OF THE FEATHERS

WHAT International Pillow Fight Day

WHERE Around the world

DETAILS Feathers were flying as a massive crowd bopped each other with pillows. More than a hundred cities participated in the event, which was held to encourage people to get off their rumps and play.

WOMAN TURNS INTO SODA MACHINE

WHAT Human vending machine

WHERE Tokyo, Japan

DETAILS How do you hide if a monster is chasing you down the street? Disguise yourself as a vending machine, of course! Fashion designer Aya Tsukioka created a layered skirt that doubles as a hiding place. When you lift the top layer in front of your head, it looks like a soda machine to hide behind. Let's just hope the monster doesn't crave a bubbly beverage.

BLINGED-OUT BENZ

WHAT Crystal-covered cars

WHERE Chiba, Japan

DETAILS Someone went a little crazy with the glue gun. A luxury auto company embellished two cars—one painted silver and the other gold—with 300,000 crystals. Each. The cars, worth about a million dollars apiece, were on display at the Tokyo Auto Salon. Pedestrians, get out your sunglasses!

PIE IN THE SKY

WHAT Sky-high restaurant

WHERE Brussels, Belgium

DETAILS Whatever you do, don't drop your silverware. Dinner in the Sky lifts its diners, table, and waitstaff about 160 feet into the air for a meal. Guests are strapped to their seats the entire time. Although based in Belgium, the restaurant can be driven almost anywhere. Next stop, space?

FROZEN FOOD

WHAT Chilly chili-eating contest

WHERE Hangzhou, China

DETAILS Hot or cold? How about both! Participants in this contest tried to eat as many hot peppers as they could—while sitting in barrels of ice water. The winner ate 62 peppers in three minutes and earned a gold bar as his trophy. Bet he'll never order hot sauce again.

STRAW MAN

WHAT Straw bears

WHERE Heldra, Germany

DETAILS Somebody went overboard with their winter coat. In colder months, some Germans have a tradition of wearing outfits made of straw while attending seasonal festivals. These "straw bears" date back to an old belief that the outfits would scare winter away. All this guy needs is a straw scarf.

1

The **closest black hole** to Earth is about **1,000 light-years** away.

2

A black hole's **gravity** is **so strong it pulls in** nearby material—including **stars**—and **"eats" it.**

3

Supermassive black holes are more than a **million times larger** than the sun.

4

It took **eight telescopes** working around the world **at the same time** to **capture the first image** of a black hole in 2019.

5

Black holes eventually **evaporate** until there is **nothing left.**

6

Black holes are the **only objects** in **the universe** that can **trap light.**

7

If you **fell into** a black hole, you'd stretch **like a noodle**—which scientists call **spaghettification.**

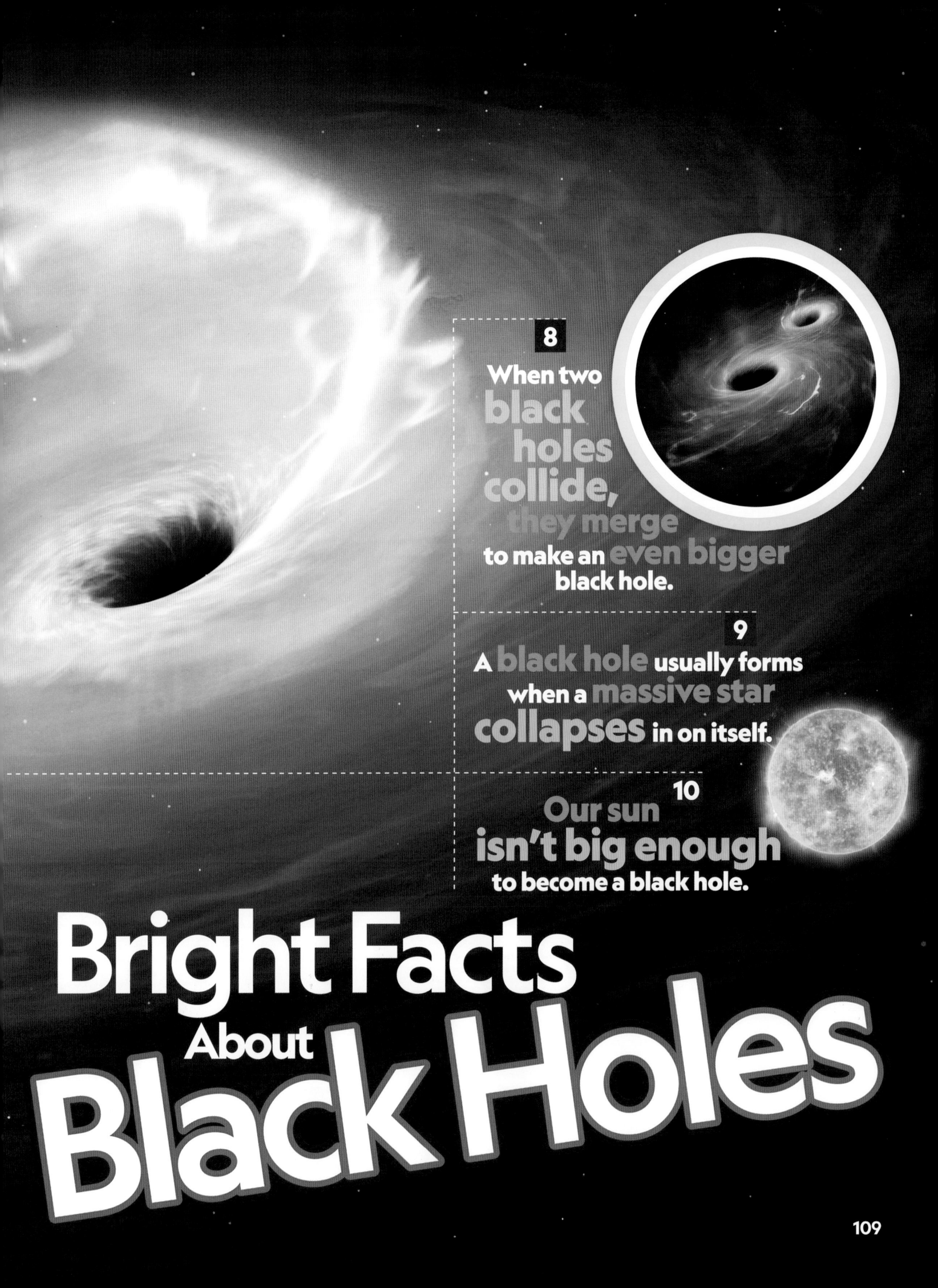

8

When two black holes collide, they merge to make an even bigger black hole.

9

A black hole usually forms when a massive star collapses in on itself.

10

Our sun isn't big enough to become a black hole.

Bright Facts About Black Holes

Check Into These Facts About Cool Hotels

1

At North Shire in England, visitors can stay in the **Dorm Room Cottage,** which is modeled on the **Gryffindor** dormitories from the Harry Potter series.

2

At the Cristalino Lodge in Brazil, you can view **birds and monkeys** in the Amazon rainforest canopy from two 165-foot (50-m)-tall towers.

3

Guests at two hotels in Austria can **sleep outside** in repurposed concrete **drainage pipes.**

4

The Henn na Hotel in Tokyo, Japan, employs a **robotic dinosaur** to **greet guests** and check them into their rooms.

5

Every April, you can view the **northern lights** from **heated igloo pods** at the North Pole.

6

You can stay overnight in an abandoned **lighthouse** in Long Island Sound with views of **New York City's** skyline.

7

Guests at the Dog Bark Park Inn in Cottonwood, Idaho, U.S.A., can sleep in the "muzzle" of a **two-story-tall house** that looks like a **beagle.**

8

Hotel owners transformed a 1965 Boeing **727 airplane** into a **two-bedroom lodge** that looks like it's flying out of a Costa Rican **rainforest.**

9

At a hotel overlooking Capertee Valley in Australia, guests stay in secluded, **see-through bubble** tents **perfect for stargazing.**

10

Canada's Hotel de Glace **features rooms and beds carved out of ice.**

1

Owls **can't move their eyes.**

2

Soaring at the cruising altitude of a **commercial airplane,** the Ruppell's griffon vulture is the **highest-flying bird** in the world.

High-Flying Facts About Birds of Prey

3

The **bald eagle's call** is more of a **chuckle** than a mighty cry, so in movies **it's dubbed over** with the piercing screech of a **red-tailed hawk.**

4

The **peregrine falcon** is the **fastest animal** in the world, with a top speed of 200 miles an hour (322 km/h), three times **faster than a cheetah.**

5

From the air, kestrels can spot **lines of urine** their prey left on the ground.

6

Vultures can eat meat **so rotten** it would **make other animals sick.**

7

A **bald eagle nest** in Florida, U.S.A., weighed almost **three tons** (2.7 t)– about as much as 30 adult men.

8

Vultures pee on their legs **to cool off** when it's hot.

9

Barn owls **swallow** their prey **whole.**

10

Scientists think the **great horned owl's** long, **hornlike tufts** of feathers help **camouflage** the bird in trees.

Colorful Facts About Coral Reefs

1

Coral are **soft-bodied animals related to jellyfish** and anemones.

2

The box jellyfish has thousands of **stinging cells** on its tentacles, making it the **most venomous** marine animal.

3

Bargibant's **pygmy seahorse camouflages** itself so well in its coral home that it went undiscovered until 1969.

4

Hawaiian squirrelfish defend their hiding spots inside reefs by **grinding their teeth,** which sounds like a **chattering squirrel.**

5

Brain coral gets its name because its shape and **grooved surface** look like a human brain.

6

The piano fangblenny, a type of coral reef fish, **eats the mucus** of **other fish.**

7

Hawksbill turtles use their **pointed beaks** to **feast on sponges** that grow on coral reefs.

8

Coral gets its color from the **algae** that live **inside it.**

9

Coral use **tentacles** to **capture prey.**

Turn the page for more cool coral facts!

10

Scientists study coral fossils to learn about what the weather was like during prehistoric times.

11

Sponges that live on coral reefs produce chemicals that help fight human infections, including cancer.

12

Coral reefs make up just one percent of the ocean floor.

13

Coral reefs are home to about 25 percent of all marine life.

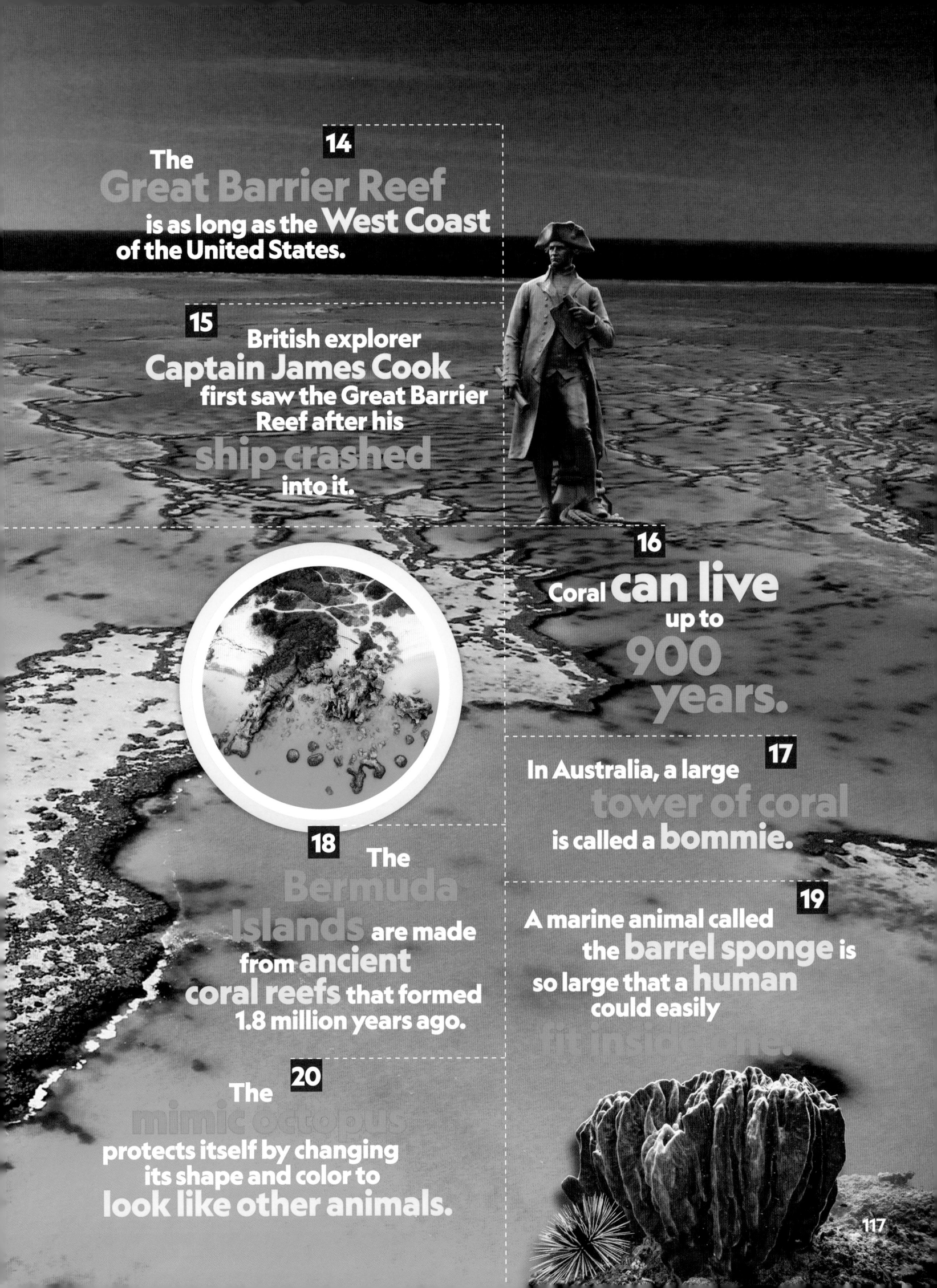

14

The **Great Barrier Reef** is as long as the **West Coast** of the United States.

15

British explorer **Captain James Cook** first saw the Great Barrier Reef after his **ship crashed** into it.

16

Coral **can live** up to **900 years.**

17

In Australia, a large **tower of coral** is called a **bommie.**

18

The **Bermuda Islands** are made from **ancient coral reefs** that formed 1.8 million years ago.

19

A marine animal called the **barrel sponge** is so large that a **human** could easily **fit inside it.**

20

The **mimic octopus** protects itself by changing its shape and color to **look like other animals.**

1

When the **RoboCup** competition was founded in 1997, the goal was to **have robots** advanced enough to **beat the best** human soccer players by 2050.

2

In the 1980s, **kids from** the island of **Koh Panyee, Thailand,** built a **floating soccer field** made out of wood.

3

About **250 million** people play soccer worldwide, making it the world's **most popular sport.**

4

The **first game with a ball** was played in Mesoamerica some 3,000 years ago—**the ball** was made from **tree resin.**

5

The **World Cup trophy** was first kept in a **bank vault** between World Cups, but it's now housed at the **FIFA World Football Museum** in Zurich, Switzerland.

6

A British man once set a world record by spending more than **48 hours** straight playing a **soccer video game.**

Get a Kick Out of These Soccer Facts

7

In 1314, **King Edward II** of England **banned soccer** in London, citing **the noise** created when large groups of people kicked and threw a ball in the city.

8

The **top goal scorer** in every World Cup final receives the **Golden Boot** award.

9

Today, soccer balls are **filled with air,** but early versions were filled with **hair and feathers.**

10

It's said that in the early 1900s, a **soccer league** in the United States **paid its players 35 cents a goal.**

Naturally Pricey Facts

1

The rare **taaffeite** (pronounced tar-fite) gem—**only a handful** have ever been found—**sells for $2,500** for a single carat.

2

In 2014, a security guard protected the **world's largest white truffle** as it was flown from Italy to New York, U.S.A., where the more than **four-pound** (2-kg) **mushroom** sold for $61,000.

3

Some **meteorites** can fetch as much as **one million dollars per pound** (0.5 kg).

4

About two pounds (1 kg) of **vanilla beans** can cost **$400.**

5

In 2002, seven-tenths of an ounce (20 g) of Da Hong Pao **tea** sold at auction for $28,000; these rare tea leaves come from a single group of trees of which only a few remain.

7

Used to treat brain tumors in humans, venom from the **deathstalker scorpion** sells for as much as $39 million per gallon because it is very difficult to harvest.

6

One pound (450 g) of the spice **saffron** can cost as much as $5,000—it's so expensive because each tiny thread of the spice is hand-gathered from saffron crocus flowers.

8

A three-foot (1-m)-long piece of what was thought to be 20-million-year-old **fossilized poop** sold for more than $10,000. (It was later found to be fossilized plant matter.)

9

Hard-to-find **red diamonds** rarely sell for less than $100,000.

10

Abandoned **swiftlet nests,** which are made with the bird's saliva and used in a delicacy called **bird's nest soup,** can cost as much as $1,000 per 2.2 pounds (1 kg).

1

The sun has **enough energy** to burn for about **five billion more years.**

2

Pluto is **not very big**— only half as wide as the United States.

3

You could fit **one million Earths** inside **the sun.**

4

The **Milky Way galaxy** is orbiting a **giant black hole** that is surrounded by about **10,000 more** black holes.

5

Jupiter is more than **twice as big** as all the other **planets combined.**

6

The winds on **Neptune** travel faster than the **speed of sound.**

Surprising Facts About the Solar System

7

When an asteroid is captured by a planet's gravitational pull, it can become a moon of that planet.

8

Some asteroids are hundreds of miles wide, while others are as small as pebbles.

9

The solar system is about 4.5 billion years old—young compared to the more than 13-billion-year-old universe.

10

Sometimes rocks from Mars crash into Earth after asteroid strikes knock them off the red planet.

Say G'Day to Awesome Facts About Australia

1

The **Australian Alps** have more area covered in snow than Switzerland's Alps.

2

The quokka, a marsupial found on Rottnest Island, Australia, has been labeled the "happiest animal in the world."

3

There are more than twice as many kangaroos as there are humans in Australia.

4

Australia is the only continent on Earth without an active volcano.

5

Koalas, which live in Australia's eucalyptus forests, get most of the water they need from eating leaves.

6

During a melon festival in Chinchilla, Australia, people ski down a hillside using watermelons as the skis.

7

Mount Disappointment in Wandong, Australia, was named for the disappointing view at its peak.

8

The northwestern tip of Tasmania, an island state of Australia, has the cleanest air in the world.

9

Bacteria and algae turn Western Australia's Lake Hillier bubblegum pink during the summer.

10

Australia is home to 21 of the 25 most venomous snakes in the world.

1

Apollo 13 astronauts used **duct tape** to repair the air filtration system on their spacecraft during their troubled 1970 mission—a life-saving remedy.

2

Police use the fumes from warmed **superglue** to make fingerprints visible.

3

Fish scales can be used to make glue.

4

Velcro became popular after NASA used it inside space helmets for astronauts to scratch their **noses.**

5

Resin, the sticky stuff that oozes from trees, is an ingredient in some **toothpastes.**

6

The sea hare—a species of **sticky slug**—can weigh 30 pounds (14 kg).

7

Our lungs produce about **three ounces** (100 mL) **of mucus** per day—about as much as a small juice box—to trap germs.

Facts That Will Stick With You

8

Elmer's glue has a cow on the bottle because the glue was once made from milk.

9

A frog's ultra-sticky tongue can snag insect prey faster than a human can blink.

10

A substance based on the slime that hagfish spew to clog predators' gills might one day be used as a protective coating for divers.

What's the Difference?

Check out these similar pairings and see how you can determine this from that!

BUTTER VS. MARGARINE

Butter and margarine are both pale yellow and can be spread on toast. They are essential ingredients for bakers and cooks everywhere. But while they may look and taste similar, their makeup is different. Butter is a dairy product, made by churning cream or milk. Shaking and turning the cream or milk causes the fats and liquids to separate, leaving thick, rich butter. Humans have been eating butter made from the milk of goats and sheep—and later cows—for 10,000 years. We use it to flavor our pancakes and to oil our pans before frying up eggs. Margarine didn't make its way into the kitchen until 1869, when a French chemist found a cheaper way to make a buttery product from beef fat mixed with vegetable oils. (Today's margarine leaves out the beef fat.) Margarine is naturally white, and to make it appear more "buttery," yellow coloring is added. During World War II, when butter was scarce, Americans began buying more margarine. Today, both are popular. There is debate over which one is healthier because each contains different types of fats. Cooks and bakers tend to split the difference, keeping both stocked in their kitchens.

SASQUATCH VS. YETI

It's time to play "Name That Cryptid." What's a cryptid? That's just a fancy term for legendary animals that people claim to have seen, but for which we don't have fossils, dead bodies, or live animals to prove they exist. Both sasquatch and yeti are terms for large, hairy creatures that make their homes in dense forests. The difference between them comes down to location. Sasquatch—also known as Bigfoot—is a creature said to be seen in the Pacific Northwest of North America. The yeti—also called the Abominable Snowman—is said to be spotted in the Himalaya in Asia. Some people say that sasquatch is more apelike, while the yeti is more like a bear.

Yeti

Hail

FREEZING RAIN VS. SLEET VS. HAIL

Icy drops are falling. Is it freezing rain, or sleet, or hail? When rain falls through a thin layer of cold air, the drops don't have enough time to completely freeze. That's freezing rain. If the layer of air is thicker, the drops have enough time to freeze into sleet before hitting the ground. Hail, on the other hand, happens when a raindrop high in a cloud starts to freeze and then is pushed upward by strong winds, hitting more water droplets as it rises. As the process repeats itself, the pellet gets bigger and bigger until it is too heavy to stay aloft. Then, watch out! You can get walloped with hail the size of a small pea or a large softball.

CRICKET VS. BASEBALL

Grab a bat and a ball and get ready to play! But which sport—a rowdy game of cricket or a rousing game of baseball? Both are team sports, and in both games, players try to hit balls to score runs while the opposing team tries to get players out so they don't score. In cricket, bowlers throw balls to try to knock two small horizontal pieces called bails off the top of three sticks called wickets, and batters try to stop the bails from getting knocked down. In baseball, pitchers throw balls past batters who try to hit the balls and then run around four bases. Another difference—scores in baseball rarely go above 20, but in cricket they can be in the hundreds.

Cricket

BACTERIA VS. VIRUSES

Bacteria and viruses are both microbes—tiny living things that are so small you can't see them without a microscope. But other than being mini, these two kinds of microbes don't have much in common. Bacteria live almost everywhere on Earth, even in our bodies. There are about as many bacterial cells in your body as human cells. The fact that you are crawling with bacteria isn't bad, though. Most of them help keep you healthy. These good bacteria digest food, make vitamins, and keep out bad bacteria that make you sick. For example, bad bacteria can give you strep throat and ear infections. But medicines called antibiotics can kill these bacteria. Viruses also cause a lot of diseases. They cause mild ones, like the common cold, and serious ones, like COVID-19 and measles. Unfortunately, antibiotics don't work on viruses, but vaccines can prevent many illnesses that viruses cause. And washing your hands can help prevent the spread of both bad bacteria and viruses. Bring on the bubbles!

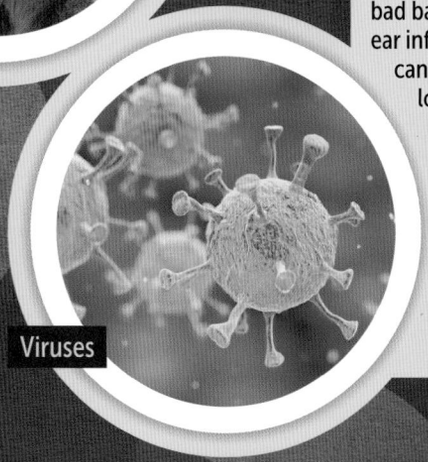

Viruses

JAGUAR VS. LEOPARD VS. CHEETAH

It's not always easy to tell the difference between a leopard, a jaguar, and a cheetah. However, a few basic facts can help single out these spotted big cats. Jaguars are usually dark yellow in color, but they can be brown or even black. Their fur has spots called rosettes because the pattern—a big spot surrounded by smaller spots—looks like a rose. Jaguars are stocky and more muscular than leopards or cheetahs, but they are the shortest of all the big cats. They live mostly in South America. Leopards look a lot like jaguars, but they are smaller (though not shorter). Their rosettes are smaller and form a closer cluster. Leopards live in Africa and Asia. Cheetahs have solid black spots on tan fur. They are the fastest land animal, built for speed with slender bodies and long legs. Cheetahs live in Africa and parts of Iran. Can you spot the differences now?

1

The tiny globe skimmer dragonfly migrates **11,000 miles** (17,700 km) back and forth across the Indian Ocean—**the longest migration of any insect**—to follow the seasonal rainfall it needs in order to reproduce.

2

Bar-headed geese have **extra-large lungs** and more efficient breathing to help them **migrate over the Himalaya,** the world's highest mountain range.

3

The arctic tern has the longest recorded **round-trip migration,** a 44,000-mile (70,811-km) route that zigzags from **Antarctica to Greenland.**

4

Each year, the U.S. Forest Service closes two roads in the Shawnee National Forest in southern Illinois, so timber **rattlesnakes, copperheads,** and **cottonmouth** snakes can **migrate safely** to their summer feeding grounds.

5

Each year, the bar-tailed godwit **crosses the Pacific Ocean** from Alaska, U.S.A., to New Zealand in a nine-day **nonstop flight,** without food or drink.

6

Migrating **monarch butterflies** roost in trees at night, and each year's new generation **roosts in the same areas** as the previous year's butterflies.

Moving Facts About Migration

7 **Zooplankton** float each night to the ocean's surface to feed, and then return to deep water in the morning to hide from predators.

8 As many as **10 million** straw-colored fruit bats darken the skies in Zambia's Kasanka National Park between October and December each year to feast on fruit trees.

9 Scientists think birds take hundreds of daily **"power naps,"** lasting only a few seconds each, to make up for lost sleep during long migrations.

10 No single monarch butterfly **lives long enough** to make an entire migration; it takes four or five generations to complete the journey.

Facts About Rulers Who Reigned Supreme

1

Britain's **Queen Elizabeth II** celebrates her birthday **twice:** once on her actual birthday in April, and again in June when the **weather is better.**

2

Fifteenth-century European ruler **Vlad III Dracula** is believed to be **the inspiration** for the famous **fictional vampire.**

3

In medieval England, Queen Elizabeth I served **gingerbread men** that looked like her **distinguished guests.**

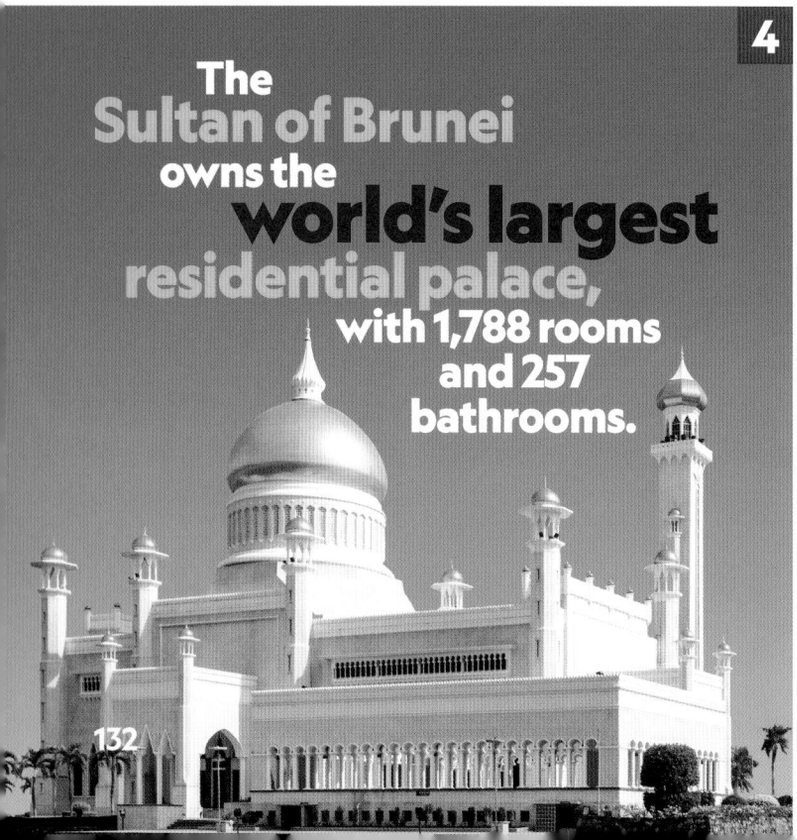

4

The **Sultan of Brunei** owns the **world's largest residential palace,** with 1,788 rooms and 257 bathrooms.

5

In the 1970s, **Queen Margrethe II** of Denmark illustrated the Danish edition of ***The Lord of the Rings.***

6

In the 13th century, King Henry III of England kept a **polar bear,** which hunted for fish in the River Thames.

7

Iolani Palace, the **only royal palace** in the United States, was home to the last ruling monarchs of what was until 1895 the Kingdom of Hawaii.

8

King Tutankhamun (or King Tut) has been nicknamed Egypt's Boy King because his **reign began** when he was **nine years old.**

9

In Britain, **all swans** without designated owners belong to the queen.

10

Albert II, Prince of Monaco, has competed in five **winter Olympics** in bobsledding.

1

Elephant calves sometimes **suck their trunk** for comfort, like human kids **suck their thumb.**

2

An **elephant's trunk** is strong enough to **push down a tree.**

3

Asian elephants sometimes **hold branches** in their trunks to **swat flies** away.

4

Some elephants—called big tuskers—grow **extra-long tusks** that **touch the ground.**

5

An elephant's **trunk** can hold two gallons (7.6 L) of water—as much as **32 glasses** of liquid.

6

African elephants' ears are **shaped like** the **African continent.**

7

An African elephant's **heart weighs** up to **46 pounds** (21 kg).

8

An elephant can use hundreds of **subtle signals** and movements—like curling its trunk or folding its ear—**while playing** with other elephants.

9

Elephant **tusks never stop** growing.

10

Elephants sometimes **greet each other** by **wrapping their trunks** together.

Exceptional Facts About Elephants

Gold Rush

Facts to Dig Into

1

California was not the site of the first American gold rush— North Carolina was.

2

In 1799, a 12-year-old boy in North Carolina found a 17-pound (8-kg) gold nugget.

3

His dad used it as a doorstop before a jeweler recognized it as gold, and the gold rush began.

4

In 1857, a ship carrying 3,100 gold coins, more than 80 pounds (36 kg) of gold dust, and 45 gold bars from the California gold rush sank off the coast of South Carolina— the recovered treasure is worth more than $50 million today.

5

During the Klondike gold rush in Canada, a scam artist set up fake telegraph poles and wires and took prospectors' money to "wire" messages home.

6

Blue jeans were invented as **sturdy work pants** for gold rush **miners in California.**

7

At the height of **California's gold rush,** as gold diggers came to the state and **farmers had trouble** meeting food demands, a single chicken **egg could cost $1—** the equivalent of about **$30 today.**

8

The **San Francisco 49ers,** named for the **1849 gold rush,** have won five Super Bowls.

10

Rabbit Creek in Yukon, Canada, was renamed **Bonanza Creek** after **gold was found** there in 1896.

9

It's estimated that almost **$2 billion worth of gold** was mined during the **California gold rush.**

1

A tree-dwelling ant from Southeast Asia **explodes** when attacked, **spewing its enemies** with sticky, **toxic goo.**

2

When threatened, some sea cucumbers **poop out their guts,** which **entangle predators.** (The organs quickly regenerate.)

3

The potato beetle **eats a plant** that is **poisonous to its predators** and then coats itself in its **poisonous poop.**

4

Wolverine frogs **break their own bones** and then poke them through their skin to **use as claws.**

5

When some **wasps are threatened,** they give off a **chemical alarm** that calls other wasps to come help sting the attacker.

6

With just **one kick** of its foot, the cassowary, an Australian bird, **can slice open a predator** using a **four-inch-long** (10-cm) **claw.**

7

The shock of an **electric eel** could **knock a horse** off its feet.

8

One type of lizard **shoots blood from its eyes** when threatened to confuse predators and to give the lizard **a chance to escape.**

9

Porcupines charge backward into predators because their sharp **quills point backward.**

10

Tarantulas sometimes spin **"trip wires"** over their burrows to **alert them** to prey passing overhead.

Sharp and Stinging

Facts About Animal Defenses

1 Some scientists believe that ancient **Egyptian astronomers** used stars' positions in the sky to **align the Pyramids** at Giza to true north.

2 The Great Pyramid of Giza is **the only** one of the **Seven Wonders** of the Ancient World **still standing.**

3 The **2,000-year-old** Great Pyramid of Cholula, located in what is now Mexico, is as wide as **nine Olympic swimming pools** but lies hidden under trees, grass, and soil.

4 **Sudan has more** pyramids **than Egypt.**

5 The **Pyramid of the Sun,** built by ancient Mesoamericans, has a **network of tunnels** under it that lead to a chamber that may have been used for funeral rituals.

6 Some Egyptians who built the pyramids **were paid** in **radishes, onions,** and **garlic.**

7 When a 16th-century **Spanish explorer** saw the Chavín temple, an ancient flat-topped pyramid in Peru, he thought it was created **by giants.**

Ancient Facts About Pyramids

Chichen Itza

8

Sudan pyramids have **elephants and giraffes** etched on their bases, which shows that the desert was once a **lush grassland.**

9

The **Maya and Aztec** built pyramids on top of their **older pyramids.**

10

If you **clap your hands** at the base of the Chichen Itza pyramid, it sounds like a flock of **chirping birds.**

1 Modeled after **termite mounds,** an office building in Zimbabwe has **holes** that allow the structure to draw in cool air and expel hot air.

2 Fish fins, which are as sensitive as **human fingertips,** could help scientists improve the ability of **underwater robots** to explore the oceans.

3 Scientists are developing a **painless needle** for shots based on a **mosquito's stinger.**

4 Scientists are designing underwater sensors, based on the frequencies **dolphins** use to **communicate,** to transmit **tsunami warnings** from deep in the ocean back to land.

5 Scientists are learning how to make strong, **nontoxic glue** based on the **sticky substance mussels use** to attach themselves to rocks and boat bottoms.

Mind-Blowing Facts About Biomimicry

6

A new type of window glass is clear to humans but looks like a spiderweb to birds, which keeps them from flying into the glass and getting hurt.

7

A tiny beetle in the Namib desert that collects moisture in grooves on its back and channels the moisture to its mouth is a model for engineers on how to harvest water from the air.

8

Scientists at Stanford University, in California, U.S.A., climbed walls using hand and foot attachments based on gecko feet, which contain an adhesive that grips tight but releases easily for the next step.

9

The flexible wings of the rose butterfly, which must absorb sunlight to fly, inspired a super-efficient design for solar cells.

10

A company in Colombia made a firm but flexible backpack based on the overlapping shells on an armadillo's back.

Strange Places

Blue Volcano

When a volcano on the tiny Indonesian island of **Krakatau erupted** in August 1883, it could be heard **thousands of miles away.**

More than 10 million people live in Jakarta—Indonesia's city with the **largest population.** That's about **two million more** people than are living in New York City.

A strange eruption creates a dazzling light show.

The night is pitch-black. But the dark slopes of a hill inside the crater of Kawah Ijen volcano in Indonesia, a country in Asia, are lit up like a holiday light show. Tourists flock to the volcano to see what look like glowing blue rivers of lava. But they aren't rivers of lava. They're rivers of glowing sulfur.

BURNING BLUE

Glowing red lava flowing from an erupting volcano isn't unusual. Glowing sulfur is. Hot, sulfur-rich gases escape constantly from cracks called fumaroles in Kawah Ijen's crater. The gases cool when they hit the air. Some condense into liquid sulfur, which flows down the hillside. When the sulfur and leftover gases ignite, they burn bright blue and light up the night sky. Scientists were told that sulfur miners on the volcano sometimes use torches to ignite the sulfur. The blue flames make Kawah Ijen popular with tourists, who watch from a safe distance. Recently scientists confirmed that some of the sulfur and gases also burn naturally, igniting as hot gases combine with oxygen in the air.

VOLCANO MINERS

Sulfur is a common volcanic gas, and its chemical properties are used to manufacture many things, such as rubber. But it's so plentiful in Kawah Ijen's crater that miners make a dangerous daily trek into the crater to collect sulfur from a fumarole near an acid lake. They use ceramic pipes to move the gases from the fumarole. Then they spray the pipes with water from a spring. This cools the gases and causes them to condense into molten sulfur. The sulfur then cools and hardens into rock. Using this method, miners get more usable rock faster than if they just collected scattered pieces. They smash up the rock with metal bars, stuff the pieces into baskets, and carry them out of the crater on their backs. The loads are heavy—between 100 and 200 pounds (45 to 91 kg) apiece.

READING THE DANGER ZONE

Miners face another danger: a huge eruption. Kawah Ijen's last big eruption was more than 200 years ago, but the volcano is still active. A big eruption could endanger hundreds of miners and tourists. Indonesian scientists want to find a way to predict a big eruption in time to keep everyone safe. But the deep acid lake makes it difficult to pick up the usual signals that warn of a coming volcanic eruption. For example, certain gases are usually more abundant right before an eruption. But in this lake, those gases dissolve in the deep water before they can register on the geologist's monitoring equipment. As scientists search for ways to predict this unusual volcano's behavior, Kawah Ijen's blue fires continue to attract audiences who appreciate the volcano's amazing glow.

HOW KAWAH IJEN ERUPTS

Earth's outer shell is broken into a jigsaw puzzle of several tectonic plates, or gigantic slabs of rock, that move constantly. In Indonesia, the oceanic Australian plate slips under the Eurasian plate at a subduction zone. As the Australian plate slides deep down, heat generated in Earth's interior makes the plate superhot, and parts of it melt. This melted rock, called magma, rises toward Earth's surface. Pressure on the magma lessens as it rises, allowing gases inside to expand, which can lead to explosive volcanic eruptions.

More than **70 active volcanoes** are in Indonesia.

Indonesia is a group of more than **17,500 islands** off the coast of Southeast Asia. It is the largest country in the region.

Penguin Facts in Black and White

1

Little blue penguins, also called **fairy penguins,** are the world's **smallest penguins** at only about 13 inches (33 cm) tall.

2

Adélie penguin **poop, colored pink** from the krill they eat, is so bright scientists can **see it from space.**

3

A **colony of penguins** is called a **waddle** when it's on land and a **raft** when it's in the water.

4

A now extinct **giant penguin** was as big as **an adult human.**

5

One colony of **chinstrap penguins,** located in the Sandwich Islands, contains more than **a million breeding pairs.**

6

A male emperor penguin's **brood pouch—** where he **holds the egg** on top of his feet—**is 100°F** (38°C) inside, while the outside air is minus 30°F (-34°C).

7

Galápagos penguins **hold their flippers over their toes** to keep their webbed feet from getting **burned** by the hot sun.

8

New Zealand's Fiordland crested penguins, or tawakis, nest under rocks and fallen trees—they are the **only penguins** that **live in rainforests.**

9

An **emperor penguin once dove** to **1,850 feet** (564 m)—most emperor penguin dives are only to about 650 feet (198 m).

10

There are **no penguins** at the **North Pole.**

Terrific Facts About Turning Trash Into Treasure

1

An artist built Cabana Floripa—a **two-bedroom house** in Florianopolis, Brazil—from old wood, pieces of mirrors, glass bottles, and pottery left over from **demolished local houses.**

2

Upcycle food is **food scraps** made into **tasty dishes,** like a pizza company in Brooklyn, New York, U.S.A., that uses **bruised vegetables** to make sauces.

3

Mount Trashmore in Cedar Rapids, Iowa, U.S.A., offers trails and a **scenic overlook** on a **mountain** made of **compacted trash.**

4

A company in Nairobi, Kenya, takes **old flip-flops** and uses them to create artwork such as **4.5-foot-tall** (1.4-m) **giraffes.**

5

Plastic bottles can be **turned into yarn** used to make puffy jackets, pants, and shoes.

6

Craftspeople turn **old plastic bags** into **reusable tote bags,** mats to sleep on, and decorative baskets.

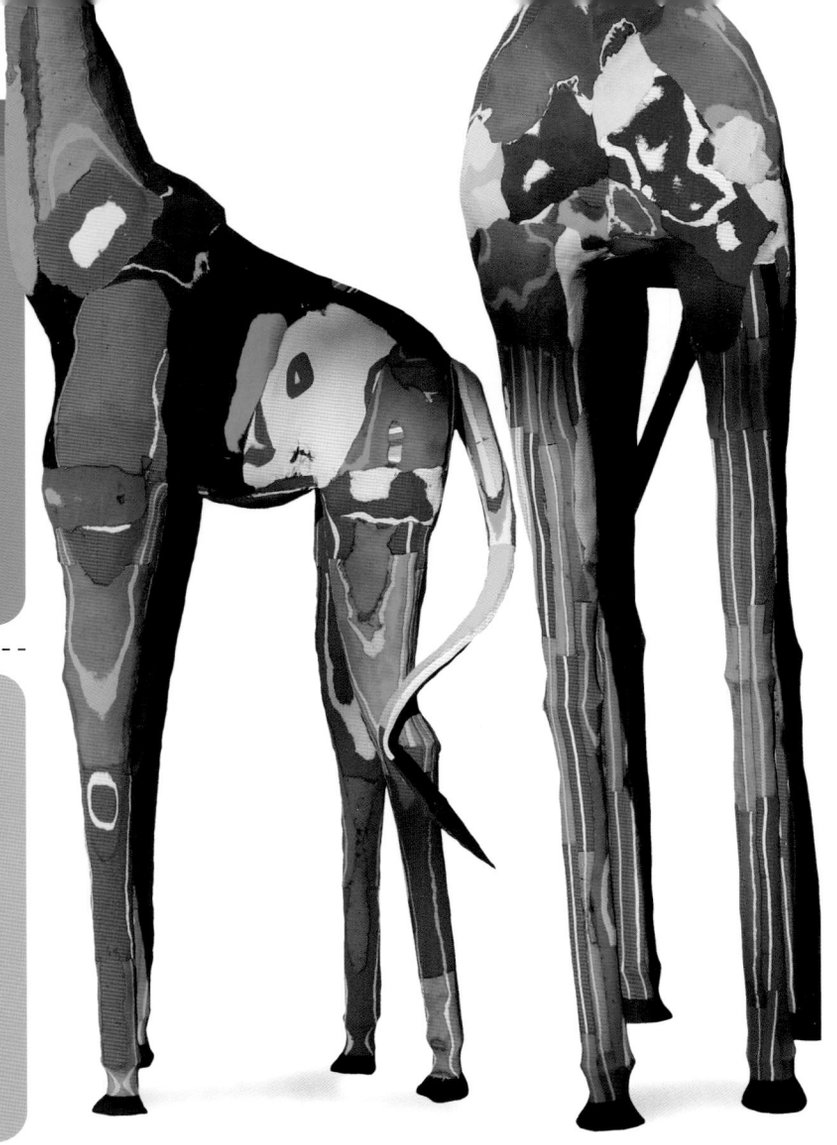

7

Old **coffee or tea cups** can become **bird feeders** or **birdbaths.**

8

Colorful paper from **old magazines** can be rolled up to create **decorative bowls.**

9

Visitors to **Magic Gardens** in Philadelphia, Pennsylvania, U.S.A., walk along paths with walls embedded with **bicycle parts, glass bottles, mirrors,** and other reused trash.

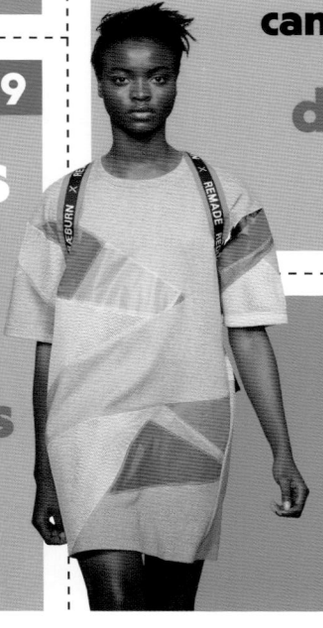

10

A designer in London uses surplus **army parachutes** to create **fashionable clothes.**

Perplexing Facts About Puzzles and Codes

1 Code breakers at Bletchley Park in Britain solved the Germans' **Enigma code,** which experts think **shortened World War II** by at least **two years.**

2 Tony Fisher, a British puzzlemaker, built a **five-foot** (1.5-m)**-tall Rubik's Cube** using the same materials as in the handheld version.

3 President Thomas Jefferson **developed a code** using the keyword **"artichokes"** so that Meriwether Lewis could **send secret messages** during the 1804–1806 expedition to map part of the American Northwest—but there is no evidence it was ever used.

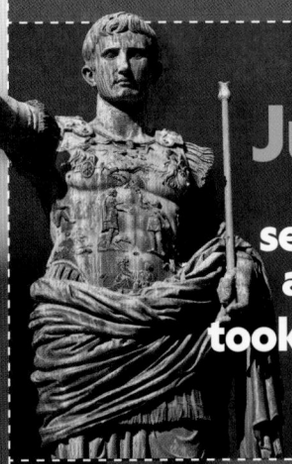

4 Roman leader **Julius Caesar** shifted letters by a set number to create a coded message that took some **800 years to crack.**

5 **"Fun"** was the number one "across" answer in the world's **first crossword puzzle,** which was created by a *New York World* journalist in 1913.

6 The **"Kryptos" sculpture,** located at the Central Intelligence Agency's headquarters outside Washington, D.C., contains an **encrypted message**—and one small part remains undeciphered.

7 There are **255,168 ways** to fill out a **tic-tac-toe** game board.

8 The Culper **spy network** operated during the **American Revolution** to pass information about the British to General George Washington—the spies wrote in **invisible ink** and used a **number system** to identify one another.

9 In 1762, the **first jigsaw puzzle** was made by mounting a **map of England** on a piece of wood and cutting out the counties for kids to reassemble.

10

Written in the 1400s, the Voynich manuscript uses **an alphabet nobody** has been able to **understand.**

Catchy Facts About

Famous Musicians

1

In 2005, **Paul McCartney** became **the first musician to broadcast a concert into space** when it was transmitted to the International Space Station.

2

Prince liked **the color purple** because it represented **royalty,** and had a song and album with "purple" in the title.

3

Taylor Swift grew up on a **Christmas tree farm.**

4

Queen singer **Freddie Mercury** dedicated his solo album **to his cats.**

5

Before she sings, **Selena Gomez** sometimes takes **a sip of olive oil—** she says it helps her voice.

6

Dolly Parton once **lost** in a Dolly Parton **look-alike contest.**

7

The cries of **Jay-Z's newborn daughter Blue Ivy** appear on his song "Glory."

8

A lock of **Elvis's hair** sold for **$115,000** in 2002.

9

Elton John has a **walk-in closet** to store his **sunglasses.**

10

Six years before *Hamilton* opened on Broadway, **Lin-Manuel Miranda** rapped an **early version** of one of its songs for President Barack Obama **at the White House.**

Zany Facts About Zoos

1 China gifted Washington, D.C.'s Smithsonian National Zoo two **giant pandas** after U.S. president **Richard Nixon** visited the country in 1972.

2 At the San Diego Zoo in California, U.S.A., giraffes eat **real acacia leaves** hung high in **fake trees.**

3 On hot days at some zoos, big cats are given **"bloodsicles,"** or blocks of **frozen blood,** to chew on.

4 Omaha's Henry Doorly Zoo in Nebraska, U.S.A., is home to the world's largest **indoor swamp**—and nine American alligators—under a **13-story dome.**

5 An Asian **elephant** named Lucky celebrated her **60th birthday** with a **large cake** made of fruits and vegetables at the San Antonio Zoo in Texas, U.S.A.

6 **Koko,** a western lowland gorilla born at the San Francisco Zoo in California in 1971, learned how to **communicate** with sign language.

7

Giraffes at Taronga Zoo in Sydney, Australia, were given wreaths covered in **foliage** and **apples** as a **Christmas treat.**

8

A school of **poop-eating** tilapia fish help keep the 70,000-gallon (265,000-L) **hippo pool** clean at the Cincinnati Zoo in Ohio, U.S.A.

9

Flamingos at Zoo Miami in Florida, U.S.A., were **sheltered** from a **hurricane** in a restroom.

10

New York City's Bronx Zoo set a world record in 2016 with its display of **78,564 origami elephants.**

Dig These Facts About Fossils

1

A **fossilized bone** doesn't contain any bone—over many years, the bone has **turned to rock.**

2

One huge coprolite—**fossilized poop**—was **17 inches (43 cm) long** and 6 inches (15 cm) wide and thought to be a dropping from a ***Tyrannosaurus rex.***

3

Paleontologists call **fragments** of dinosaur bones **too broken up to identify** "chunkasaurus."

4

Some mythological creatures, such as **centaurs, griffins,** and **cyclops,** may have been **inspired by fossils.**

5

Scientists can tell **how much** an **animal weighed** by studying its fossilized **footprints.**

6

The American Museum of Natural History in New York City stores fossils in a **10-story building**—seven of those stories contain **only dinosaur bones.**

7

Paleontologists discovered the fossil of a **three-foot-tall** (1-m) **parrot** and named it **Squawkzilla.**

8

While walking on a beach in England in 2009, **five-year-old** Daisy Morris found a fossil of an **unknown pterosaur**—scientists named it *Vectidraco daisymorrisae* after her.

9

Scientists found 3.5-billion-year-old **fossilized bacteria** in Australia that may be the **oldest known life** on Earth.

10

Dinosaur fossils have been found on **every continent,** and about **50 new species** are discovered **each year.**

Extreme Weirdness

VADER RULES THE SKY

WHAT Hot-air balloon festival

WHERE León, Mexico

DETAILS This might be the Rebels' worst nightmare. Participants at this festival soared across the sky in giant hot-air balloons, such as this one shaped like Darth Vader's mask. More than a hundred balloons fly each year—anything from pandas to bees to scarecrows. But don't worry. This Vader's only full of hot air.

WOMAN WALKS ON AIR

WHAT Art illusion

WHERE Lodz, Poland

DETAILS Look out below! Artist Regina Silveira of Brazil specializes in creating optical illusions. Her piece, titled "Depth," makes it look as if she's floating inside a tall building. A digitally generated image on the flat floor makes it seem as if the room extends several stories below her feet. That's some smart art.

COZY CLUCKERS

WHAT Sweaters for hens

WHERE Norwich, England

DETAILS Word on the farm is that wool sweaters for chickens are all the rage. People across England knitted "woolly jumpers" for rescued hens that had lost feathers from stressful living conditions. About 1,500 hens were fitted with sweaters of all designs—stripes, bows, and even a few holiday themes.

BLOOMS ON WHEELS

WHAT Flower parade

WHERE Zundert, Netherlands

DETAILS What's that smell? Flowers—lots of them. Every year some 50,000 people head to this Dutch town to see an elaborate parade of petals. In addition to giraffes and other animals, the floats are shaped like giant monsters, cityscapes, motorcycles, ships, and yes, even flowers. Best-smelling parade ever.

BIGGEST HAT EVER

WHAT Ice-cream carton headgear

WHERE Ascot, England

DETAILS Some people eat out of ice-cream cartons—this woman wears them. Huge hats are popular at Royal Ascot, an English horse racing event. Among the hats worn by the crowd was this gigantic one, made of gold spray-painted ice-cream cartons. Wonder what she did with all that ice cream?

TREE STOPS TRAFFIC

WHAT Traffic light tree

WHERE London, England

DETAILS Money doesn't grow on trees—but traffic lights might! This 26-foot (8-m)-high treelike structure is made of 75 sets of traffic lights controlled by computers. The sculpture, created by a French artist to represent the energy of the city around it, has been a big hit with locals. Sounds like this fake tree has really taken root.

Facts About

Famous Firsts

1

The first **McDonald's hamburger,** made in 1948, cost 15 cents.

2

The **first airplane,** the Wright Flyer, was in the air for only **12 seconds** on its first flight.

3

In 1895, **Annie Londonderry—** who had never ridden a bicycle before— became the **first woman** to **ride around the world** on one.

4

The first **box of crayons,** sold in 1903, had **only eight colors:** black, brown, blue, red, purple, orange, yellow, and green.

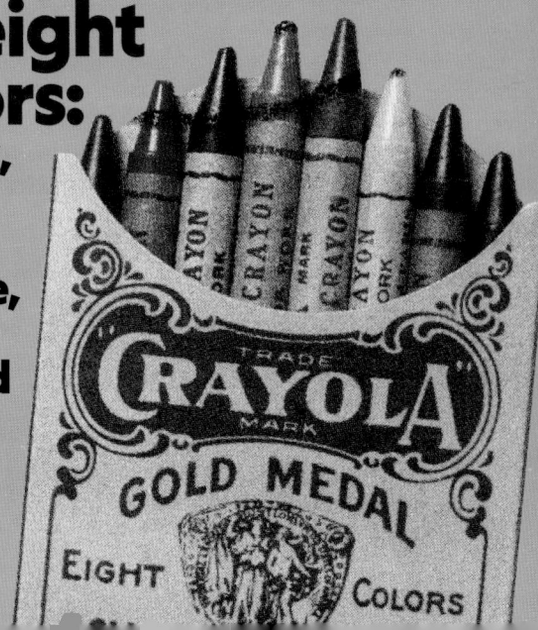

5

The first **text message** was **"Merry Christmas."**

6

Astronaut **Buzz Aldrin** took the first **space selfie** in 1966 while on the Gemini 12 mission.

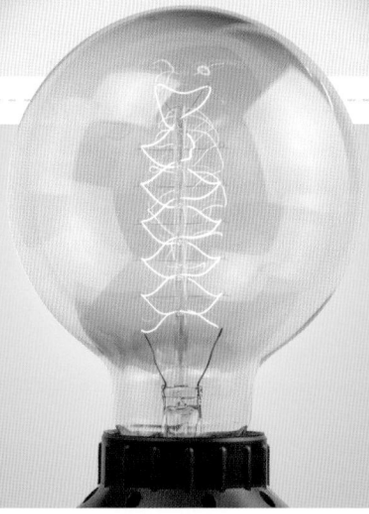

7

When **electric lights** were first installed in the **White House,** in 1891, President Benjamin Harrison and his wife, Caroline, refused to touch the switches for fear of **getting shocked.**

8

When scientist Robert Plot discovered the first **dinosaur bone** in 1677, he thought it was the bone of a **giant human.**

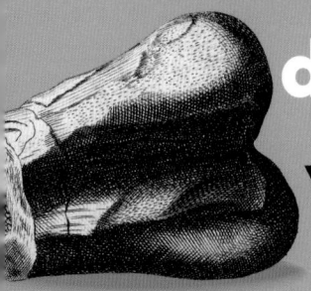

9

The **first cell phone weighed 2.5 pounds** (1.1 kg), about **six times the weight** of today's smartphones.

10

Victoria Woodhull ran for United States **president** almost **50 years before a** constitutional amendment gave women **the right to vote.**

1

Maglev trains use **magnetic fields** to **levitate trains above the tracks,** allowing them to travel at high speeds.

2

In Japan, professional **"subway pushers"** pack passengers into **crowded trains.**

3

New York City buses **don't accept paper money** because the giant vacuum hoses used to empty the fare boxes would **shred the bills.**

4

The **largest bus** in the world is 72 feet (22 m) long, can **carry 300 passengers,** and has three segments so it can bend on tight turns.

5

Parts of some **train wheels** were once **made of paper.**

Rev Your Engine
With These Facts About
Vehicles

6

Engineers in Slovakia built a **car** that can **transform into** an **airplane.**

7

After a man **wrecked his car** in the desert in Morocco in 1993, he built a **functioning motorcycle** out of the **car parts** and rode it to safety.

8

The first **cars did not have steering wheels;** they were guided by joystick-like levers.

9

In Britain, **ghost trains** sometimes run **without passengers.**

10

Some airplanes have **hidden bedrooms** where the **flight crew sleeps** during long flights.

What's the Difference?

Check out these similar pairings and see how you can determine this from that!

IGNEOUS VS. SEDIMENTARY VS. METAMORPHIC ROCK

All rocks are not created equal. Rocks are classified into three groups: igneous, sedimentary, and metamorphic. Igneous rocks form when magma, or molten rock, slowly cools underground or when lava—magma that erupts from a volcano—cools on Earth's surface. Sedimentary rocks form when small bits of sand, rock, and mud accumulate in layers that fuse together over time. Metamorphic rocks have been changed from the extreme pressures deep in Earth's depths or by the motion of tectonic plates on the surface. Rocks can change form. For example, wind and water can erode igneous rocks into smaller pieces that are then deposited into layers that slowly turn into sedimentary rocks. If these rocks are pushed deep below Earth's surface, they become metamorphic rocks. Cool!

Emu

Metamorphic rock

CLEMENTINES VS. TANGERINES VS. SATSUMA MANDARINS

Tangerines, clementines, and Satsuma mandarins all are members of the mandarin orange family. Clementines are the smallest and are seedless. They're known for their smooth, glossy peel and deep red-orange color. They sometimes go by the nicknames "cuties" and "sweeties" in the grocery store. Tangerines have a rougher, thinner skin, making them a little harder to peel. They're bright orange and more tart than clementines, with a few seeds. Satsuma mandarins, which were first grown in Japan 700 years ago, are a lighter orange. They're sweet and generally seedless. Their claim to fame is that they are the easiest variety to peel, but they're also more fragile and can damage easily if squished. Another thing all three share? They are chock-full of vitamin C!

Bee

Tangerine

EMU VS. OSTRICH

While these big birds may look alike, they're worlds apart. Emus are found mostly in Australia, but also in New Guinea, Indonesia, the Solomon Islands, and the Philippines. Ostriches live in African savannas and deserts. Though emus and ostriches may never cross paths, they do have plenty in common. For example, neither bird can fly, but both are quick on their feet. Emus can run up to 30 miles an hour (48 km/h). Ostriches can run up to 43 miles an hour (69 km/h), and they use their wings as "rudders" to steer and change direction while running. Both ostriches and emus have powerful legs. An ostrich kick is strong enough to kill a lion. And emus are the only bird with calf muscles! But these birds of a feather have one big difference—their size. An emu tips the scales at 100 pounds (45 kg), but that's nothing compared to the ostrich, which weighs up to 350 pounds (159 kg). It's the biggest bird on the planet.

WASP VS. HORNET VS. BEE

Wasps, hornets, and bees are all insects. But they have important differences, too. Wasps have a pointy end and a narrow "waist" that separates the two parts of their bodies. Some wasps are solitary, while others are social. Solitary wasps use their stinger to hunt other insects. Social wasps use their stinger only for defense. Hornets are a type of wasp, but they are usually a little bigger and fatter than most other wasps. All hornets are social. They chew wood into papery pulp and then use that pulp to build hives. They eat flies, bees, and other insects. Like other social wasps, hornets use their stinger only for defense. A single wasp or hornet can sting many times. Bees are rounder and plumper than wasps and have hairy bodies and legs. They collect pollen from plants. Like social wasps, bees use their stinger just for defense, but they can only use it once: They die after delivering a sting.

ANTHROPOLOGY VS. ARCHAEOLOGY

What kind of scientist is likely to get really dirty on the job—an anthropologist or an archaeologist? Both academic disciplines study human beings. Anthropology is the study of human cultures—past and present. It includes the study of human biology, as well as how modern humans fit in among all the species on the human family tree. Anthropology also includes linguistics, the study of language. Archaeology is a branch of anthropology. It's the study of past cultures, which includes excavating ancient places such as the Pyramids of Giza in Egypt to learn about what these people believed and how they spent their days.

STALACTITE VS. STALAGMITE

It's no wonder people confuse stalactites and stalagmites—they're only separated by two letters! While these two cave features are similar in their outward appearance, they are formed differently. Luckily, there's a handy way to remember how to tell them apart. A stalactite hangs from the ceiling or sides of a cave like a giant icicle. It is commonly cone-shaped with a pointed tip and forms when water containing minerals from the cave's limestone rock walls slowly drips down. A stalagmite is the opposite of a stalactite. It looks like a spear with a rounded or flattened tip rising from the cave's floor. A stalagmite forms slowly over time as drips from a stalactite hit the floor. Sometimes a stalactite and stalagmite will connect and form a column. Still confused over which is which? Try this alphabet trick: Stalactite is spelled with a *c,* as in "ceiling"—it hangs from the ceiling. Stalagmite has the letter *g,* as in "ground"—it extends up from the ground.

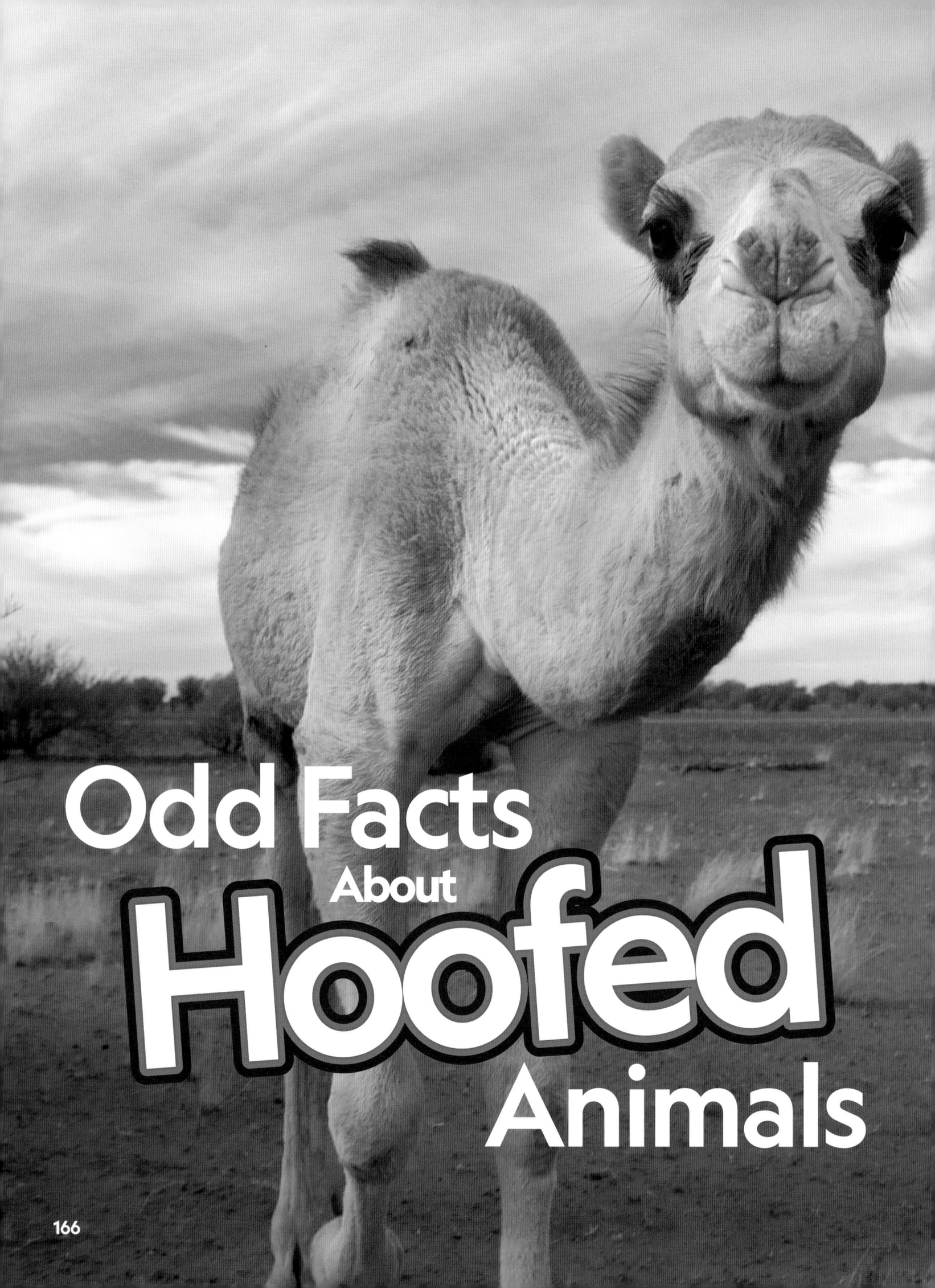

Odd Facts About Hoofed Animals

1 Camels have two rows of extra-long eyelashes to keep out the desert sand.

2 The hippo's closest living relative is the whale.

3 Mother pigs sing to their babies.

4 A tapir uses its snout as a snorkel when swimming underwater.

5 Horses can't vomit.

6 A group of giraffes is called a tower.

7 When a goat is "kidding," it is giving birth—not telling a joke.

8 American bison, which can weigh up to 2,000 pounds (907 kg), are very agile and can jump high fences.

9 Some people believed that okapis were unicorns until scientists in the early 1900s identified the wary rainforest animal as the giraffe's only living relative.

10 The pattern of a zebra's coat confuses flies, making it hard for them to land.

1

Running the bases of a baseball diamond is a longer distance than running the length of a **football field.**

2

Major league **umpires** are required to **wear black underwear** in case their pants tear.

3

At the **swimming pool suite** at the Arizona Diamondbacks' stadium, paying guests can **go for a dip** while watching the game.

4

Every new major league **baseball** is **rubbed with mud** from a secret location along the Delaware River before it is used.

5

The first **baseball caps** were **made from straw.**

Baseball

Facts That Hit It Out of the Park

6 A regulation **baseball** has **108 stitches.**

7 The average major league **baseball** is used for only **seven pitches.**

8 Instead of playing nine innings as we do today, baseball teams in the **early 19th century** played until **one team scored 21 runs.**

9 About **19 million hot dogs** are sold at major league baseball games every year.

10 In 1976, the **Chicago White Sox wore shorts** for three of their games, but switched back to pants after **players complained** of scraping their legs when **sliding into base.**

Engaging Facts About Europe

1

Bulgarians shake their heads for "yes" and nod their heads for "no."

2

Eighty-four percent of the British population **drinks tea** every day.

3

A **tooth, thumb,** and **finger** of astronomer **Galileo Galilei** are on display at the Galileo Museum in Florence, Italy.

4

In Spain, when **a child loses a tooth,** a mouse named **El Ratoncito Pérez** comes and leaves a gift under their pillow.

5

A bridge in Istanbul, Turkey, **connects** the continents of **Asia** and **Europe.**

6

There are **five times** more **bicycles than cars** in Copenhagen, Denmark.

7

In **cold weather,** the **Eiffel Tower** in Paris, France, **shrinks** approximately **six inches** (15 cm), but expands again when it gets warm.

8

More **chocolate** is sold in Belgium's **Brussels Airport** than anywhere else in the world.

9

There are **no mosquitoes in Iceland.**

10

Norway has **knighted three penguins,** all named Nils Olav.

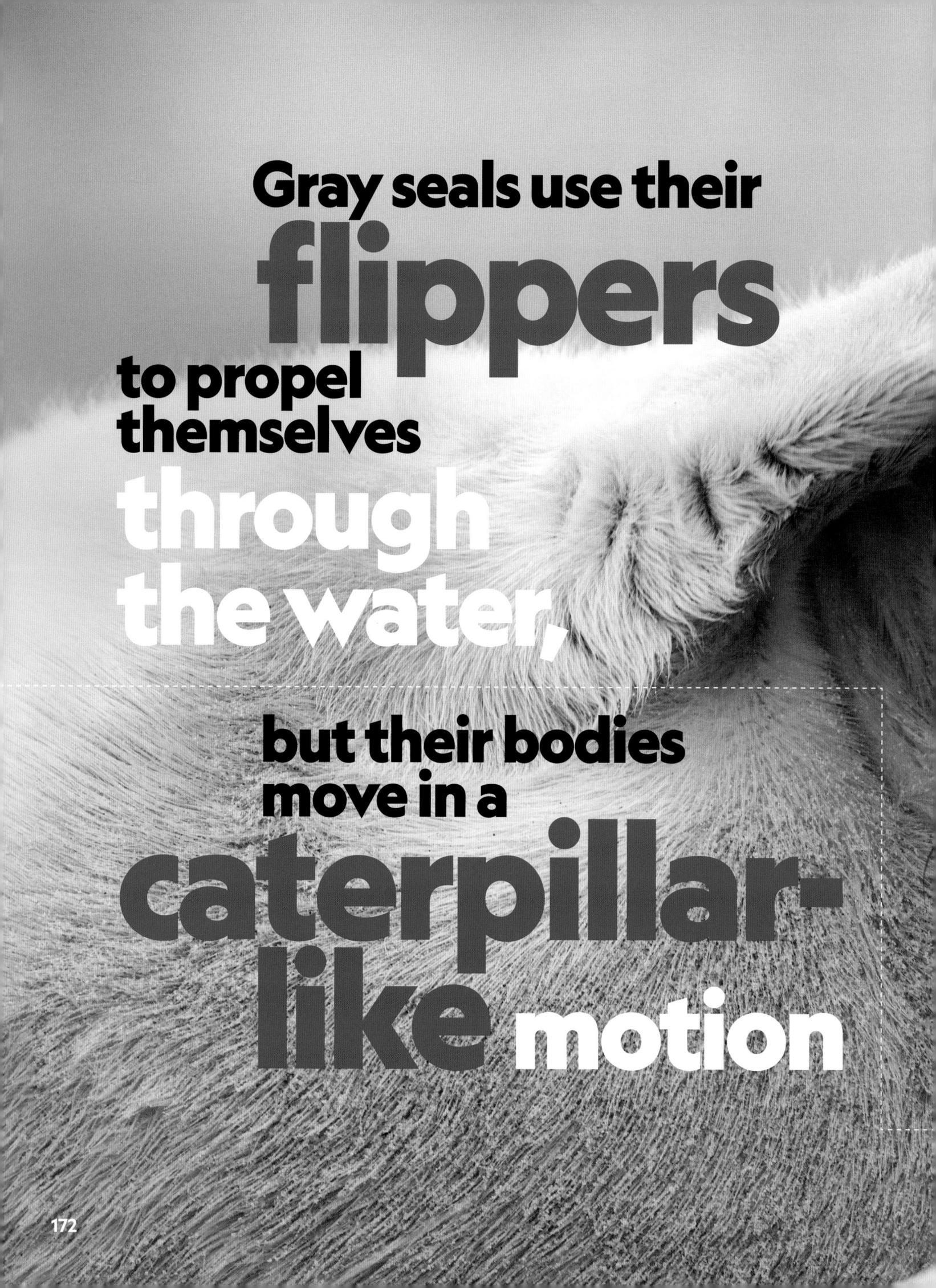

Gray seals use their **flippers** to propel themselves **through the water,** but their bodies move in a **caterpillar-like motion**

on land.

Cinematic

Facts About the Silver Screen

1 In 1975, the movie *Jaws* became the first film to earn more than $100 million at the U.S. box office.

2 The first "moving pictures" were a series of photographs that showed horses galloping and birds flying.

3 At K9 Cinemas in Plano, Texas, U.S.A., you can bring your dog to the movies.

4 President Dwight D. Eisenhower watched more than 200 Westerns in the White House movie theater during his presidency.

5 The earliest movies were silent, and when sound was added the movies became known as "talkies."

7

IMAX cameras have been into **space**, to the deepest part of the **ocean** and to the top of **Mount Everest.**

8

The **helicopter** landing pad on *Tis*, a designer yacht, can be transformed into an **outdoor movie theater.**

9

People watch movies on a grassy lawn surrounded by **graves** at the Hollywood **Forever Cemetery** in Los Angeles, California, U.S.A.

6

Before movies had sound, **popcorn wasn't allowed** to be eaten in theaters.

10

Sun Pictures in Broome, Australia, is the world's **oldest open-air movie theater,** showing movies outside since 1916.

Precious Facts About Presidential Pets

1 John F. Kennedy's dog Pushinka was the pup of one of the **first dogs** sent **into space.**

2 William McKinley had a **parrot** that could whistle **"Yankee Doodle."**

3 Warren G. Harding hosted a **birthday party** for his dog **Laddie Boy** at the White House.

4 Calvin Coolidge's pet raccoon wore a collar with the name **"White House Raccoon"** embroidered on it.

5 During World War I, **Woodrow Wilson** kept a **flock of sheep** on the White House lawn.

6

Lyndon B. Johnson's **beagles were named Him and Her.**

7

When Theodore Roosevelt's son Archie was sick, **his pony** was brought up to **his bedroom** in the White House for a visit.

8

Abraham Lincoln let his two **pet goats,** Nanny and Nanko, ride in the **presidential carriage.**

9

Herbert Hoover's family adopted a wild **opossum** that strayed onto the White House grounds and **named it Billy.**

10

William Taft's **pet cow,** which provided milk for the first family, was named **Pauline Wayne** and lived on the White House grounds.

1

A **sea urchin's** spines **help it move** along the seafloor.

2

The thistle's flower grows **spiny leaves** to protect itself from being **eaten by wildlife.**

3

A **jackfruit,** which is a yellow-green fruit with spiky skin, can weigh up to **100 pounds** (45 kg).

4

Prickly pear cactus is sometimes **used as a fence** to keep livestock from escaping.

5

The Spanish ribbed newt pokes its **sharp ribs through its skin** to **defend itself.**

6

A **crown-of-thorns starfish** can **regrow** up to half of its body if damaged.

7

When threatened, a potto bends its head to reveal **sharp vertebrae—** the primate can remain in this position for hours.

8

A porcupine's **quills are soft** when it's born, **but they harden** within a few days.

9

The **armadillo lizard rolls into a ball** when threatened, protecting itself with spines on its head and tail.

Prickly Facts That Stick Out

10 Most species of **pufferfish,** which contain enough toxin to kill 30 humans, are **covered with small spines** that stick out when the animals **inflate.**

Scientists think that young humpback whales "whisper" to their mothers so that the pair

doesn't attract the attention of nearby orcas, or killer whales.

Behind the Facts

We're sure you're wondering how we got so many awesome facts about so many awesome topics into this book. First, we came up with a list of all the coolest and most interesting things out there—things we know kids want to know more about. Like captivating critters. Pirates. Toys, holidays, and bugs. Crazy hotels. Black holes. Cookies. The future. All kinds of stuff. Then we found 10 or 20 of the most exciting and surprising facts about those topics to arrange on each page. We carefully researched each and every fact to make sure it's absolutely true, and then we packed the book full of cool bonus content! Things like strange places, moments of extreme weirdness around the world, and a feature called "What's the Difference?" that will answer age-old questions like "What's the difference between a porcupine and a hedgehog?"

And we designed the pages so colorfully that you'll pore over them endlessly and will love flipping to all your favorite parts. And one last fact: It took a big team of writers, editors, photo researchers, and designers to make this book—the greatest book team around!

Illustration Credits

AL = Alamy Stock Photo; AS = Adobe Stock; DR = Dreamstime; GI = Getty Images; IS = iStockphoto; MP = Minden Pictures; SS = Shutterstock

Cover (terraced fields), Emilio JoseG/SS; (aurora borealis), SurangaSL/SS; (Great Wall of China), Liusheng Film/SS; (doughnut), Demkat/SS; (sun), Triff/SS; (Great Barrier Reef), Marco Brivio/AS; (hedgehog), praisaeng/AS; (gold nugget), Uros Petrovic/AS; (quokka), Kevin Schafer/The Image Bank RF/GI; (sundew plant), Julie DeRoche/Design Pics/GI; (elephants), Johan W Elzenga/IS/GI; (Venus flytrap), Cathy Keifer/IS/GI; (Eiffel Tower), Dan Breckwoldt/DR; Spine (quokka), Kevin Schafer/The Image Bank RF/GI; Back cover (hippo), Gubin Yury/SS; (watermelon), vhpfoto/SS; (cheese), Tim UR/SS; (bald eagle), Jason/AS; (Egyptian pyramids), Volker Kreinacke/AS; (ladybug), jaroslav kettner/AS; (blue crystals), jonny sek/AS; 1, James Keith/GI; 2-3, Ron and Patty Thomas/GI; 4 (UP), KevinHyde/iStock/GI; 4 (UP CTR), Sergey Gorshkov/MP; 4 (LO CTR), demphoto/AS; 4 (LO), Natee K Jindakum/SS; 5 (UP), Tui De Roy/MP; 5 (UP CTR), zhaojiankang/iStock/GI; 5 (LO CTR), Willee Cole/GI; 5 (LO), Stanislav Moroz/AL; 6 (UP LE), DmitriiK/AS; 6 (UP RT), John W Banagan/GI; 6 (LO LE), Henner Damke/SS; 6 (LO RT), Dr Morley Read/SS; 6 (BACKGROUND), Charnchai Saeheng/DR; 7 (UP), VW Pics/GI; 7 (LO), Kevin Schafer/MP; 8 (LE), SciePro/IS/GI; 8 (RT), Panther Media GmbH/AL; 9 (UP), Master Photo 2017/SS; 9 (CTR), Samuel B./AS; 9 (LO LE), 7activestudio/IS/GI; 9 (LO RT), SciePro/IS/GI; 10, rimglow/IS/GI; 10 (BACKGROUND), Stocktrek Images/GI; 11 (UP LE), World History Archive/Newscom; 11 (UP RT), NASA/SIPA/Newscom; 11 (LO), NASA/CampoAlto/V. Robles; 12 (UP), simoneemanphoto/AS; 12 (CTR LE), StevenEllingson/IS/GI; 12 (CTR RT), Imgorthand/GI; 12 (LO LE), Historic Images/AL; 12 (LO), Alp Aksoy/SS; 13, paulista/age fotostock; 14, ido Meirovich/GI; 14-15, Stanislav Moroz/AL; 15 (UP), Kiwipic/IS/GI; 15 (LO), Tui De Roy/Nature Picture Library/AL; 16 (UP), Sunny/IS/GI; 16 (CTR), tpuerzer/IS/GI; 16 (CTR), Eliks/SS; 16 (LO LE), Mary Terriberry/SS; 16 (LO RT), Grassetto/IS/GI; 17, GoodFocused/SS; 18, Tom & Pat Leeson/age fotostock; 18-19, Sergey Gorshkov/MP; 19 (UP), Patricio Robles Gil/MP; 19 (LO), BearFotos/SS; 20 (UP LE), MediaProduction/GI; 20 (UP RT), Alexey Novikov/DR; 20 (CTR), sharrocks/IS/GI; 20 (LO LE), Arthur Edwards/The Sun/PA Images/AL; 20 (LO RT), Thearon W. Henderson/GI; 21 (UP LE), Njnightsky/DR; 21 (UP RT), Photocreo Bednarek/AS; 21 (CTR), Bettmann/GI; 21 (LO LE), JoKMedia/IS/GI; 21 (LO RT), andresr/GI; 22 (UP), Michel Gunther/MP; 22 (LO LE), RooM The Agency/AS; 22 (LO RT), Arm001/SS; 23 (UP), JOEL SARTORE/National Geographic Image Collection; 23 (CTR), Masato Hattori/Science Source; 23 (RT), LPA/Dave Pressland/age fotostock; 24 (UP), Miroslav Hlavko/DR; 24 (LO LE), Fairfax Media/GI; 24 (LO RT), Joel Sartore/National Geographic Image Collection; 25 (UP LE), Thomas Marent/MP; 25 (CTR), Jason Bazzano/AL; 25 (LO LE), Lorraine Bennery/MP; 25 (LO RT), Buiten-Beeld/Jelger Herder/AL; 26 (UP LE), murat bingöl/IS/GI; 26 (UP RT), Gerard Koudenburg/AL; 26 (LO LE), vgajic/IS/GI; 26 (LO RT), Svetlana Foote/DR; 27 (UP LE), Granger, All rights reserved; 27 (UP RT), Richard Watkins/AL; 27 (CTR), harmoony/IS/GI; 27 (LO LE), Artem/AS; 27 (LO RT), xamtiw/IS/GI; 28, Jef Meul/MP; 30 (UP), Maks Narodenko/SS; 30 (LO LE), 4kodiak/IS/GI; 30 (LO RT), fcafotodigital/IS/GI; 31 (UP), reativeNature_nl/IS/GI; 31 (UP CTR), LindaHughesPhotography/AL; 31 (CTR), DanielBendjy/IS/GI; 31 (LO CTR), Charlotte Lake/AL; 31 (LO), Sergiy Kuzmin/GI; 32 (UP), Jasmina007/GI; 32 (CTR), Marco Bottigelli/GI; 32 (CTR RT), Liliboas/IS/GI; 32 (BACKGROUND), Dudarev Mikhail/SS; 33 (LE), buradaki/IS/GI; 33 (RT), Pawan Kumar/Reuters; 34 (UP LE), Stanislau_V/AS; 34 (UP RT), Chris Willson/AL; 34 (CTR), JHPhoto/AL; 34 (LO LE), at2foto/AL; 34 (LO LE), feellife/IS/GI; 35 (UP), Jon D/Alamy; 35 (UP CTR), ABDESIGN/IS/GI; 35 (CTR), CTRPhotos/IS/GI; 35 (LO CTR), CTRPhotos/IS/GI; 35 (LO), Ivonne Wierink/SS; 36 (UP LE), serts/IS/GI; 36 (UP RT), AP Photo/James Brooks; 36 (CTR), AnthiaCumming/IS/GI; 36 (LO LE), Pixel-Shot/AS; 36 (LO RT), New Africa/GI; 37 (UP), Gabe Palmer/AL; 37 (LO), Joe Benedict/AL; 38 (UP), Max Zvonarev/SS; 38 (LO LE), artisteer/IS/GI; 38 (LO RT), travellinglight/AL; 39 (UP), glaflamme/IS/GI; 39 (CTR), Artur Didyk/SS; 39 (LO), Oleg Zaikin/AL; 40, Ted Kinsman/Science Source; 41, ASMR/GI; 42 (UP), Steven Kovacs/Blue Planet Archive; 42 (LO), Jaap Bleijenberg/AL; 43 (UP), Alex Mustard/naturepl/Alamy; 43 (LO), Espen Rekdal/Blue Planet Archive; 44, Joe McDonald/GI; 44-45, Serjio74/IS/GI; 45 (UP), janaph/GI; 45 (LO LE), Pictorial Press Ltd/AL; 45 (LO RT), RMyers/AL;

46 (UP), Suzanne C. Grim/SS; 46 (CTR), raksyBH/IS/GI; 46 (LO), sdominick/IS/GI; 46 (BACKGROUND), Marcel Strelow/AL; 48 (UP LE), VVCephei/IS/GI; 48 (UP RT), Suradech14/IS/GI; 48 (LO), Science & Society Picture Library/GI; 49 (UP LE), The Print Collector/AL; 49 (UP RT), Daisy-Daisy/IS/GI; 49 (LO LE), inhauscreative/GI; 49 (LO RT), David Cole/AL; 49 (LO RT), FalkensteinFoto/AL; 50 (UP), robertsrob/GI; 50 (CTR), RayArt Graphics/AL; 50 (LO), DNY59/GI; 51 (UP LE), chamnan phanthong/AS; 51 (UP RT), Cavan Images/IS/GI; 51 (LO LE), sonmez/IS/GI; 51 (LO RT), i-Stockr/IS/GI; 52 (UP), Bettmann/GI; 52 (LO), Fred Hirschmann/AL; 52-53, sumikophoto/SS; 53 (UP), Fabideciria/SS; 53 (LO), Lee Rentz/AL; 54 (UP CTR), Bournemouth News/SS; 54 (LO CTR), Lisa Maree Williams/Stringer/GI; 54 (LO CTR), Mike Blake/Reuters/AL; 55, Marco Secchi/GI; 56 (UP), dszc/GI; 56 (LO), ImageBROKER/FB-Fischer/AL; 56 (BACKGROUND), zorazhuang/IS/GI; 57 (UP), Pajor Pawel/SS; 57 (LO), Rajesh Vora/Dinodia Photo/age fotostock; 58 (UP LE), Dario Sabljak/AL; 58 (UP RT), tihomir_todorov/IS/GI; 58 (LO LE), Swee Ming Young/EyeEm/GI; 58 (LO RT), Mathieu B.Morin/AL; 59 (UP LE), xjbxjhxm/IS/GI; 59 (UP RT), Allstar Picture Library Ltd/AA Film Archive/Alamy; 59 (CTR), Erik Karits/AL; 59 (LO LE), caracterdesign/GI; 59 (LO RT), George Grall/AL; 60 (UP LE), ConstantinCornel/IS/GI; 60 (UP RT), nechaev-kon/IS/GI; 60 (LO LE), Husni Che Ngah/MP; 60 (LO RT), loonger/IS/GI; 61 (UP), defun/GI; 61 (LO LE), Antagain/IS/GI; 61 (LO RT), Michael Durham/MP; 62 (UP), Voren1/IS/GI; 62 (LO), Vladimir Konstantinov/SS; 62-63, RooM the Agency/AL; 63 (UP), aydinmutlu/GI; 63 (LO), suriya silsaksom/IS/GI; 64, INTERFOTO/AL; 64-65, Angelo D'Amico/AL; 65 (UP), De Agostini Picture Library/age fotostock; 65 (LO), Catrina Genovese/GI; 66 (UP), Chuck Haney/Danita Delimont/AL; 66 (CTR), Imago History Collection/AI/AL; 66 (LO), Tim de Waele/GI; 67 (UP), sunugal/AL; 67 (LO), NASA Image Collection/AL; 67 (BACKGROUND), Jamie Squire/GI; 68, ansonsaw/IS/GI; 69 (UP LE), Pulse/Corbis/GI; 69 (UP RT), Yunaidi Joepoet/GI; 69 (CTR), Marazem/DR; 69 (LO LE), Nattika/SS; 69 (LO RT), Standret/SS; 70 (UP LE), John D. Ivanko/AL; 70 (UP RT), Ferrari/Visual/Zuma Press; 70 (CTR), Donald Iain Smith/Newscom; 70 (LO), Thannaree Deepul/SS; 71 (UP), Valentyn Volkov/GI; 71 (CTR), Cover Images/Zuma Press; 71 (LO), Francois Lenoir/Reuters; 72 (UP), Dancestrokes/SS; 72 (UP CTR), luamduan/IS/GI; 72 (CTR), strickke/GI; 72 (LO CTR), CLIPAREA/Custom media/SS; 72 (LO), Aflo Co. Ltd/AL; 73, Tui De Roy/MP; 74 (UP), Christian Musat/AS; 74 (LO), 1001slide/GI; 74-75, Hugo Alonso/age fotostock; 75 (LE), Tony Heald/MP; 75 (RT), Eric Isselee/SS; 76 (UP LE), reptiles4all/IS/GI; 76 (UP RT), Buddy Mays/GI; 76 (CTR), B. Trapp/age fotostock; 76 (LO LE), mjf795/IS/GI; 76 (LO RT), Eastmanphoto/DR; 77, Mcummings1400/DR; 78 (LE), Kham TPX/Reuters; 78 (RT), Aman Kalyan/EyeEm/GI; 78-79, zhaojiankang/IS/GI; 79 (UP LE), Daniel Prudek/SS; 79 (UP RT), Lucy Brown loca4motion/IS/GI; 79 (LO), Mitsuhiko Imamori/MP; 80 (UP), filonmar/IS/GI; 80 (LO LE), gary corbett/AL; 80 (LO RT), Natalia Harper/AL; 81 (UP LE), pepifoto/IS/GI; 81 (UP RT), Eric Isselee/SS; 81 (CTR LE), Tim Allen/IS/GI; 81 (CTR RT), Vladimirovic/IS/GI; 81 (LO LE), mychadre77/IS/GI; 81 (LO RT), Fred Bavendam/MP; 82, Leochen66/DR; 82-83, Cathy Keifer/IS/GI; 83 (UP), Nick Garbutt/Nature Picture Library; 83 (LO), VStock LLC/AL; 84 (UP), Studio Carlo Dani/age fotostock; 84 (CTR), Maxim Tarasyugin/DR; 84 (LO), Franco Tempesta/National Geographic Image Collection; 84 (BACKGROUND), Jenhuang99/DR; 85, Suzi Eszterhas/MP; 86-87, Yiming Chen/GI; 88, Westend61/GI; 88-89, Piotr Krzeslak/GI; 90 (UP), Destina/AS; 90 (LO), Zuberka/GI; 91 (UP LE), SPL/Science Source; 91 (UP RT), fortton/AS; 91 (CTR), INTERFOTO/AL; 91 (LO LE), Charles D. Winters/Science Source; 91 (LO RT), abriendomundo/GI; 92, Maria Adelaide Silva/AL; 92-93, phive2015/IS/GI; 93 (UP), adventtr/IS/GI; 93 (LO), airtime/SS; 94 (UP), Florilegius/AL; 94 (LO), Arterra Picture Library/De Meester Johan/AL; 96, Johner Images/AL; 96 (BACKGROUND), Sumio Harada/MP; 97 (UP), Gerard Soury/GI; 97 (CTR LE), Kyle Bedell/AL; 97 (CTR RT), Azure-Dragon/IS/GI; 97 (LO), Niels Poulsen std/AL; 98 (UP LE), Carolyn Jenkins/AL; 98 (UP RT), MKucova/IS/GI; 98 (CTR), Suradech14/IS/GI; 98 (LO LE), Tracey Patterson/IS/GI; 98 (LO RT), Bea Cooper/AL; 99 (UP LE), photastic/SS; 99 (UP RT), Mariah Tauge/GI; 99 (CTR), Ben Hider/GI; 99 (LO LE), Melica/SS; 99 (LO RT), Spalnic/SS; 100 (UP), Jim Zipp/Science Source; 100 (CTR), MahirAtes/GI; 100 (LO), Natalia/AS; 100 (BACKGROUND), MattStansfield/GI; 101 (UP), IgorCheri/AS; 101 (CTR), Grinf4ce/SS; 101 (LO LE), EcoPic/IS/GI; 101 (LO RT), Eric Isselee/SS; 102 (UP), Kalcutta/SS; 102 (LO), Michael and Patricia Fogden/MP; 102-103, jacobeukman/IS/GI; 103 (UP), Tom van den Brandt/age fotostock; 103 (CTR), Tom McHugh/Science Source; 103 (LO), Paulo de Oliveira/age fotostock; 104 (UP), francisblack/GI; 104 (LO), North Wind Picture Archives/AL; 104-105, FOTOGRAFIA INC./GI; 105 (UP), David Carillet/SS; 105 (CTR), Blackbeard the pirate (coloured engraving)19th century Peter Newark Historical Pictures/Bridgeman Images; 105 (LO), Hugoht/DR; 106 (UP), Laszlo Balogh/Reuters; 106 (CTR LE), Toru Hanai/Reuters; 106 (CTR RT), Toru Hanai/Reuters; 106 (LO), VCG/GI; 107, dpa picture alliance/AL; 108 (UP), EHT/Xinhua/AL; 108 (LO), Melica/AS; 108-109, Mark Garlick/Science Source; 109 (UP), Mark Garlick/Science Source; 109 (LO), lukszczepanski/AS; 110 (UP), duckycards/GI; 110 (CTR), Carol Cavendish/AL; 110 (LO), blickwinkel/AL; 111 (UP LE), AP Photo/Shizuo Kambayashi; 111 (UP RT), kickstand/IS/GI; 111 (CTR), Franck Fotos/AL; 111 (LO LE), Steven Oehlenschlager/DR; 111 (LO RT), SerkanSenturk/AL; 112, Maria_Oleinikova/IS/GI; 113, Tui De Roy/MP; 114-115, Debra James/SS; 115 (UP), Eduardo Baena/IS/GI; 115 (CTR), Alex Mustard/MP; 115 (LO), 500cx/AS; 116, Wild Horizon/Universal Images Group Editorial/GI; 116, Marco Rubino/SS; 116-117, JC Photo/SS; 117 (UP), davidf/IS/GI; 117 (CTR), Zach/AS; 117 (LO), Placebo365/IS/GI; 118 (UP), Du Yu/Xinhua/AL; 118 (CTR), Mike Kemp/Tetra Images/GI; 118 (LO), Peter Horree/AL; 118-119, Natee K Jindakum/SS; 119, Maria Hoffman/AL; 120 (UP), everythingpossible/IS/GI; 120 (CTR LE), The Natural History Museum, London/Science Source; 120 (CTR RT), Miguel Medina/GI; 120 (LO LE), Mike Segar/Reuters; 120 (LO RT), amriphoto/GI; 121 (UP LE), Directphoto Collection/AL; 121 (UP RT), Daniel Heuclin/MP; 121 (CTR LE), Photovs/DR; 121 (CTR RT), orinocoArt/age fotostock; 121 (LO LE), ArtInfo/Bridgeman Images; 121 (LO RT), defun/IS/GI; 122 (UP), PASIEKA/GI; 122 (LO), David Aguilar/NGP; 124, Jami Tarris/GI; 125 (UP), seeshooteatrepeat/SS; 125 (CTR), Mark Fitzpatrick/EyeEm/GI; 125 (LO LE), Johncarnemolla/DR; 125 (LO RT), adogslifephoto/AS; 126 (UP), Melissa King/SS; 126 (CTR LE), kostsov/GI; 126 (CTR RT), Pro-syanov/IS/GI; 126 (LO LE), playfulphoto/IS/GI; 126 (LO RT), Ekaterina43/SS; 127 (UP), Tomas_Mina/IS/GI; 127 (LO), Vicki Beaver/AL; 128 (UP), HABRDA/SS; 128 (CTR LE), subjug/GI; 128 (CTR RT), MousePotato/GI; 128 (LO LE), ratpack223/IS/GI; 128 (LO RT), css0101/IS/GI; 129 (UP), Bildagentur Zoonar GmbH/SS; 129 (LO LE), reisegraf.ch/SS; 129 (LO RT), cinoby/IS/GI; 130 (UP), Glenn Bartley/age fotostock; 130 (LO), Gillespie Photography/AL; 130 (BACKGROUND), JHVEPhoto/AS; 131 (UP), Fabian von Poser/GI; 131 (LO), Brent Stephenson/MP; 132 (LO LE), holgs/IS/GI; 132 (LO LE), Max Mumby/Indigo/GI; 132 (UP), pepifoto/IS/GI; 132 (CTR RT), velazquez/AS; 132 (LO RT), People Picture/Frank Rollitz/SS; 133 (UP), se-key/IS/GI; 133, Mlenny/IS/GI; 133, Benainous/Morvan/Gamma-Rapho/GI; 134 (BACKGROUND), sdbower/SS; 134 (UP), Chase Dekker/MP; 136 (UP), NUM LPPHOTO/SS; 136 (CTR), Lightboxx/AL; 136 (LO), KevinHyde/IS/GI; 137 (UP LE), NadinPanina/IS/GI; 137 (UP RT), Jeff J Daly/AL; 137 (CTR), Cal Sport Media/AL; 137 (LO LE), RobertKacpura/IS/GI; 137 (LO RT), Zachary Frank/AL; 138 (UP), Gary Bell/MP; 138 (CTR), Meister Photos/SS; 138, Eric Isselée/AS; 138, chaev-kon/IS/GI; 138-139, Okea/DR; 140 (UP LE), MarcelC/GI; 140 (UP RT), bergamont/IS/GI; 140 (CTR), Pius Lee/DR; 140 (LO), Michael Rooney/AL; 140 (BACKGROUND), Michael Godek/GI; 141 (LE), Pyramids And Tombs in Royal Cemetery, Meroe, Kush, Sudan Eric Lafforgue/Bridgeman Images; 141 (RT), PeopleImages/IS/GI; 142, Stastny_Pavel/SS; 142 (BACKGROUND), Jeff Mondragon/AL; 143 (LE), Shubhrojyoti/SS; 143 (RT), Cre8tive Images/SS; 144, Olivier Grunewald; 145, Tom Pfeiffer/Volcano Discovery/GI; 146, GoodOlga/IS/GI; 146 (BACKGROUND), Heike Odermatt/MP; 147 (UP), Jan Vermeer/MP; 147 (LO), Tui De Roy/MP; 148, malerapaso/IS/GI; 149 (UP), opuscule/AL; 149 (CTR), Kella Carlton/SS; 149 (LO), Chris Yates/AL; 150, Popartic/GI; 150 (BACKGROUND), Lars Hallstrom/SS; 151 (UP), Nataliya/AS; 151 (CTR), Paolo Gallo/AS; 151 (LO LE), Historic Collection/AL; 151 (LO RT), Art Collection 2/AL; 152 (UP LE), Pictorial Press Ltd/AL; 152 (UP RT), Larry Busacca/GI; 152 (LO), DNY59/IS/GI; 153 (UP LE), Okea/IS/GI; 153 (UP RT), WENN/Age fotostock; 153 (CTR), PA Images/AL; 153 (LO LE), Imeh Akpanudosen/GI; 153 (LO RT), Bettmann/GI; 154 (UP), Foreverhappy-Mee/IS/GI; 154 (LO), Carl De Souza/AFP/GI; 154-155, Constantin Stanciu/AL; 155, DanielPrudek/IS/GI; 156 (UP), Ton Bangkeaw/SS; 156 (CTR), kosmos111/SS; 156 (LO), evenfh/IS/GI; 157 (UP), Dreamframer/IS/GI; 157 (CTR), GlobalP/IS/GI; 157 (LO), Marques/SS; 158 (UP), Mario Armas/Reuters; 158 (CTR), SWNS South West News Service; 158 (LO LE), Nacho Calonge/AL; 158 (LO RT), Paul Gilham/GI; 159, Marko Beric/AL; 160 (UP), Ralf-Finn Hestoft/GI; 160 (UP), witsawat sananrum/IS/GI; 160 (LO LE), NASA; 160 (LO RT), Peregrine/AL; 161 (UP LE), urbazon/IS/GI; 161 (UP CTR), GlobalP/IS/GI; 161 (UP RT), Science History Images/AL; 161 (CTR), Paul D Stewart/Science Source; 161 (LO LE), History and Art Collection/AL; 161 (LO CTR), R. Gino Santa Maria/DR; 161 (LO RT), Bettmann/GI; 162 (UP), Rafael Macia/mauritius images GmbH/AL; 162 (CTR), MiroNovak/IS/GI; 163 (LO), WENN Rights Ltd/AL; 162-163, den-belitsky/IS/GI; 163, Emile Leray/SS; 164 (UP), Elena Popova/GI; 164 (CTR LE), Tonylshio/SS; 164 (CTR RT), smallhorse/SS; 164 (LO LE), Xurzon/IS/GI; 164 (LO CTR), Natikka/IS/GI; 164 (LO RT), LUNAMARINA/IS/GI; 165, thekopmylife/IS/GI; 166-167, Steffen & Alexandra/age fotostock; 167 (UP LE), Eric Isselee/SS; 167 (UP RT), esemelwe/GI; 167 (CTR LE), Mark_Kostich/SS; 167 (CTR RT), Eric Isselee/SS; 167 (LO), Saddako/IS/GI; 168 (UP), Alluvion Stock/SS; 168 (LO), zonch/AS; 168 (BACKGROUND), Michael Flippo/DR; 169 (UP), Hum Images/AL; 169 (LO), ncognet0/GI; 170 (UP), deepblue4you/IS/GI; 170 (LO), Irina Lepneva/DR; 170-171, Nikada/GI; 171 (UP), Preto Perola/SS; 171 (LO), PA Images/AL; 172-173, Erhard Nerger/Biosphoto; 174 (UP), World History Archive/AL; 174 (CTR), Alan Cotton/AL; 174 (LO), Tango Images/AL; 174-175, Yuval Helfman/AL; 175 (UP), NASA Photo/AL; 175 (LO), hidesy/IS/GI; 176 (UP), GlobalP/IS/GI; 176 (LO LE), Sonsedska/IS/GI; 176 (LO RT), New York Daily News Archive/GI; 177 (UP LE), White House Photo/AL; 177 (UP RT), Antagain/IS/GI; 177 (CTR), Irina K./AS; 177 (LO), miralex/IS/GI; 178 (UP), SEE D JAN/IS/GI; 178 (LO), Michelle Gilders/AL; 178-179, mirecca/IS/GI; 179, Tuned_In/IS/GI; 180-181, Tony Wu/Nature Picture Library

Index

Boldface indicates illustrations.

A

Aardvarks 101, **101**
Abominable Snowman 128, **128**
Adélie penguins 146
African clawed frogs 24
Airplanes **162-163**
  car transforming into 163
  first 160, **160**
  future 71, **71**
  hidden bedrooms 163, **163**
  as hotel 111
Albert II, Prince (Monaco) 133, **133**
Alice Springs, Australia 54, **54**
Alkali flies 40
Alligators 154
Alpacas 62
Amazon rainforest
  animal sounds 17
  Cristalino Lodge 110
  facts 6-7, **6-7**
  swimming 89
American alligators 154
American bison 12, 167
American Revolution 48, **48,** 151
Amphibians 22-25, **22-25**
Andean condors 53, **53**
Androids 72, **72**
Angel Falls, Venezuela 44
Angkor Wat, Cambodia 78
Animal crackers 98, **98,** 99
Animal defenses 138-139, **138-139**
Antarctica 53, 59
Antelope 74, 75, **75**
Anthropology 164, **164**
Ants 138
Apollo 13 mission 126, **126**
Arachnids 12, **12**
Archaeology 164, **164**
Arctic terns 130, **130**
Argonaut octopuses 81, **81**
Armadillos 143, 178, **178**
Armored devil toads 23, **23**
Art
  encrypted message in 151
  optical illusions 158, **158**
  sunbathing potatoes 54, **54**
  traffic light tree 159, **159**
  from trash 148-149, **148-149**
Arteries 72, **72**
Asia 78-79, **78-79,** 98, **98**
Assassin bugs 60
Asteroids 123, **123**
Astronauts
  CEVIS bike 67, **67**
  email 65
  future 71
  landmarks 14
  moon landing 91
  Silly Putty use 37
  spacecraft 10-11, **10-11**
  sticky facts 126, **126**
  video games 34, **34**
Atacama Desert, Chile 11, **11**
Aurochs 94, **94**
Australia 124-125, **124-125**
Axolotls 22, **22**
Ayodhya, India **92-93,** 93
Aztec 57, 141

B

Babbage, Charles 65
Bacteria 27, **27,** 50, 128, 157
Bagels 69, **69**
Bags, reusable 51, **51**
Baikal seals 88, **88**
Bald eagles 113
Balloons 90, **90,** 158, **158**
Bar-headed geese 130
Bar-tailed godwits 130
Barbie 35, **35**
Bargibant's pygmy seahorses 115, **115**
Barn owls 100, **100,** 113
Barnyard animals 62-63, **62-63**
Barrel sponges 117, **117**
Baseball 128, 168-169, **168-169**
Basketball 20-21, **20-21**
Bats 101, **101,** 131, **131**
Beaded lacewings 103
Bears 19, **19,** 76, **76,** 133, **133**
Bees 72, **72,** 83, 164, **164**
Beetles
  biomimicry 143
  Darth Vader beetle 58
  defenses 138
  diving beetles 61, **61**
  funky facts 102, **102,** 103
  hearing 61
Beihai Park, Beijing, China 44
Bellbirds 17
Beluga whales 18, **18**
Bermuda Islands 117, **117**
Berners-Lee, Tim 65, **65**
Bicycle Motocross (BMX) 67, **67**
Bicycles
  Copenhagen, Denmark 170
  facts 66-67, **66-67**
  firsts 49, **49,** 160
  powering blender 51
Bigfoot 128
Bikepacking 66, **66**
Bioluminescence 97
Biomimicry 142-143, **142-143**
Birds of prey 112-113, **112-113**
Bison 12, 167
Black holes 16, 108-109, **108-109,** 122, **122**
Black king snakes 76
Black rhinos 74
Blackbeard (pirate) 104, 105, **105**
Bladderworts 82
Blood 138, 154, **154**
Blue (color) 96-97, **96-97**
Blue jays 97, **97**
Blue jeans 137, **137**
Blue Lake, New Zealand 89
Blue volcano 144-145, **144-145**
Blue whales 19, **19,** 76
Bluebottle jellyfish 97, **97**
Bobsledding 133, **133**
Bollywood 79

Bombardier beetles 103
Bones 8-9, **8-9,** 156-157, **156-157**
Boston, Massachusetts, U.S.A. 46
Box jellyfish 115
Breakfast foods 68-69, **68-69**
Bridges 78, **78,** 170, **170**
Brine shrimp 40, **40**
Brown bears 76, **76**
Brunei, Sultan of 132
Brussels, Belgium 106, **106,** 171
Buffalo 12, **12**
Bug facts 12, **12,** 58-61, **58-61**
Buildings 142, 143, 148
Burrowing beetles 103
Buses 162
Bush babies 101, **101**
Butter 128, **128**
Butterflies 61, **130-131,** 131, 143, **143**

C

Cactus 178, **178**
Caecilians 23, **23,** 24, **24**
Caesar, Julius 151, **151**
Calendars, rocks as 15, **15**
California, U.S.A.
- facts 41
- gold rush 136, 137, **137**
- Mono Lake 2, **2-3,** 40, **41**
- Rose Bowl Parade 46, **46**
- superhero-shaped plane 54, **54**

Camels **166,** 167
Can openers 49
Canada 68, 136, 137, **137**
Canaima National Park, Venezuela 44
Candy Land 36
Cane toads 24, **24**
Canyons 52-53, **52-53**
Capybaras 6, **6**
Carbon 91
Carlsbad Caverns National Park, New Mexico, U.S.A. 52, **52**
Carnaval 54, **54**
Carnival 46
Carnivorous plants 82-83, **82-83**
Cars
- crystal-covered 106, **106**
- first 163
- in space 11
- toy 35, **35**
- transforming into airplane 163

Cassowaries 138, **138**
Caterpillars 61, **61**
Cats 17, 152
Cell phones 50, **50,** 161, **161**
Celsius, Anders 49
Cephalopods 42-43, **42-43**
Cereal 68, **68**
Chambered nautiluses 42, **42**
Cheese 26-27, **26-27**
Cheetahs 76, **76,** 113, 129, **129**
Chichen Itza, Mexico **140-141,** 141
Chickens 62, 63, **63,** 158, **158**
Chili peppers 30, **30,** 31, 106, **106**
Ching Shih (pirate) 104
Chinstrap penguins 147, **147**
Chocolate 30, **30,** 171, **171**
Chocolate chip cookies 98, **98,** 99, **99**
Cicadas 16, **16**
Cities 56-57, **56-57**
Clementines 164
Clinton, Bill 65
Clothes
- baseball 168, **168,** 169
- blue jeans 137, **137**
- for chickens 158, **158**
- future 70, **70,** 71
- shoes 20, **20,** 69, 148, **148-149**
- "straw bears" outfit 107, **107**
- from trash 149, **149,** 158, **158**
- vending machine disguise 106, **106**

Cockroaches 59, **59**
Codes and puzzles 150-151, **150-151**
Coffee beans 69, **69**
Common eider 103
Computer history 64-65, **64-65**
Contact lenses 71, **71**
Cook, James 117, **117**
Cookie Monster 99, **99**
Cookies 98-99, **98-99**
Coolidge, Calvin 176
Coprolites 121, 156
Coral reefs 114-117, **114-117**
Cows
- auroch 94, **94**
- cheese facts 26, **26**
- chewing 62, **62**
- on glue bottle 127, **127**
- presidential pets 177
- wagging tail 63

Crayola crayons 37, **37,** 160, **160**
Cricket (sport) 128, **128**
Crocodiles 76, **76**
Crown-of-thorns starfish 178
Curry, Stephen 20, **20**
Cuttlefish 42

D

Da Nang, Vietnam 78, **78**
Da Vinci, Leonardo 49, **49,** 72
Daintree National Park, Australia 45
Darth Vader beetles 58
Darwin, Charles 39
Dead Sea 14, **14,** 79
Death Valley National Park, California-Nevada, U.S.A. 41, 52
Deathstalker scorpions 121, **121**
Defenses, animal 138-139, **138-139,** 178
Dik-diks 75, **75**
Dinosaurs
- extinction 76
- fossils **156,** 156-157, **157,** 161, **161**
- relatives 63
- robotic dinosaur at hotel 111, **111**

Diving beetles 61, **61**
Diwali **92-93,** 93
Dogs
- hotel shaped like 111, **111**
- in movie theaters 174
- presidential pets 176, **176,** 177, **177**
- sounds 16, **16**

Dolphins 7, **7,** 142, **142**
Doughnuts 68, **68**
Dragon Boat Festival, Hong Kong 78

Dragonflies 60, 130
Drainage pipes, as hotel rooms 110, **110**
Drais, Karl von 67
Drones 60, 70, **70**
Dry Tortugas National Park, Florida, U.S.A. 45, **45**
Ducks 62, **62,** 103
Duct tape 126, **126**
Dugongs 18
Dung beetles 102, **102**

E

Eagles 6, **6,** 113
Ear bones 9
Earth 90, **90,** 122
Edison, Thomas 48, **48,** 92
Edward II, King (England) 119
Eggs 69, **69**
Egypt, ancient
  games 37
  King Tut 37, 133, **133**
  pyramids 56, **56,** 140, **140,** 164, **164**
  seasons 33
Eider 103
Eiffel Tower, Paris, France **170–171,** 171
Eisenhower, Dwight D. 174
Electric eels 138
Electric lights 92, 161, **161**
Elements 90–91, **90–91**
Elephants
  facts 134–135, **134–135**
  origami 155
  poop 51
  on pyramids 141
  sounds 17, **17**
  zoo animals 51, **51,** 154
Elizabeth I, Queen (England) 132
Elizabeth II, Queen (United Kingdom) 65, 132, **132**
Elmer's glue 127, **127**
Emperor penguins 147
Emus 164, **164**
Europe 170–171, **170–171**
Europium 91
Everest, Mount, China-Nepal 15, 79, **79**
Exploding ants 138
Eye color 96, **96**
Eye of the Sahara 14

F

Fairy flies 59
Fairy penguins 146, **146**
Falcons 113
Fall 32
Farms 62–63, **62–63,** 70
Fashion *see* Clothes
Feet 27, **27,** 31, 59, **59**
Fennec foxes 76, **76**
Festivals
  dragon boat festival 78
  hot-air balloon festival 158, **158**
  light facts 92–93, **92–93**
  weird 106, **106**
  see also Parades
Field hockey 72
Fingerprints 126, **126**
Finland 89
Fiordland crested penguins 147, **147**
Firsts 160–161, **160–161,** 174, **174**
Fish scales 126, **126**
Fisher, Tony 150
Flamingos 155, **155**
Flip-flops 148, **148–149**
Flowers 79, **79,** 178, **178**
Food
  baseball games 169, **169**
  breakfast foods 68–69, **68–69**
  butter vs. margarine 128, **128**
  can openers 49
  cheese 26–27, **26–27**
  chilly chili-eating contest 106, **106**
  chocolate chip cookies 48, **48**
  clementines vs. tangerines vs. Satsuma mandarins 164, **164**
  cookie facts 98–99, **98–99**
  edible games 36, **36**
  Europe 171, **171**
  firsts 160, **160**
  future 71
  hardtack 38, **38**
  M&M's 97, **97**
  movie theaters 175, **175**
  as payment for work 140, **140**
  pizza 56
  potatoes as art 54, **54**
  pricey facts 120–121, **120–121,** 137, **137**
  prickly facts 178
  rice as mortar 78
  sky-high restaurant 106, **106**
  smoothies 51
  snake cake 54, **54**
  sorbet vs. sherbet 12, **12**
  spicy facts 30–31, **30–31**
  upcycling 148
  watermelons as skis 125
Football 137, **137**
Fortune cookies 99, **99**
Fossils 156–157, **156–157**
Foxes 76, **76,** 100
Franklin, Benjamin 49
Freezing rain 128
Frigate birds 76
Frogs **22**
  African clawed frogs 24
  defenses 138
  froglets 25, **25**
  glass frogs 7, **7**
  mice riding on 33, **33**
  poisonous 23, 25, **25**
  sticky tongue 127
Fruit flies 59
Funky facts 102–103, **102–103**
Furbies 34, **34**
Future 70–71, **70–71**

G

Galápagos Islands 15, **15**
Galápagos penguins 147
Galilei, Galileo 170
Games 34–37, **34–37,** 150–151, **150–151**
Garlic 31, 100, **100**
Gates of the Arctic National Park and Preserve, Alaska, U.S.A 45

Geckos 143, **143**
Geese 130
Geysers 45, **45**
Ghost trains 163
Giant pandas 154, **154**
Giant penguins 146
Giant sequoias 15
Giant squid 42
Giant tortoises 15, **15**
Giraffes
  eyes 74, **74**
  group name 167, **167**
  on pyramids 141
  relatives 167, **167**
  in zoos 154, **154–155,** 155
Girl Scout cookies 99, **99**
Glaciers 45, 73, **73,** 88
Glass frogs 7, **7**
Glenn, John 65
Globe skimmer dragonflies 130
Gloomy octopuses 43, **43**
Glue 126, 142
Goats
  cheese facts 26
  intelligence 63, **63**
  kidding 167, **167**
  presidential pets 177, **177**
Godwits 130
Gold rush 136–137, **136–137**
Goliath birdeaters 76, **76**
Gomez, Selena 153
Gorillas **44,** 154
Grand Canyon, Arizona, U.S.A. 15, **52–53,** 53
Gray seals 172–173, **172–173**
Gray wolves 76, **76–77**
Great Barrier Reef, Australia 15, 117
Great Basin spadefoot toad 25, **25**
Great crested newts 25, **25**
Great Divide Mountain Bike Route, Canada-U.S.A. 66, **66**
Great horned owls 113
Great Pyramid, Egypt 56, **56,** 140, **140**
Great Wall, China 78, **78–79**
Greece, ancient 32, 34, 97
Green anacondas 7
Green facts (planet protection) 50–51, **50–51**
Gross facts 102–103, **102–103**

H

Hagfish 103, **103,** 127
Hail 128, **128**
Harbor porpoises 18
Harding, Warren G. 176
Hardtack 38, **38**
Harp seals 18
Harpy eagles 6, **6**
Harrison, Benjamin 161
Harrison, Caroline 161
Harry Potter series 110, **110**
Hawaii, Kingdom of 133, **133**
Hawaiian squirrelfish 115
Hawks 113
Hawksbill turtles 115
Hedgehogs 72, **72**
Helium 90, **90,** 91
Henry III, King (England) 133
Hermit crabs 81, **81**
Hiking vs. trekking 12, **12**
Hippos 75, 155, 167, **167**
Holidays 92–93, **92–93,** 106, **106**
  see also Festivals; Parades
Homo erectus 80
Honeybees 72, **72**
Hong Kong, China 78
Hoofed animals 166–167, **166–167**
Hoover, Herbert 177
Hornets 164
Horns 16, **16**
Horses 167
Hot-air balloons 158, **158**
Hot Wheels 35, **35**
Hotels 110–111, **110–111**
Houseflies 59, **59**
Hula-Hoops 34, **34**
Human ancestors 80
Human body
  bacteria vs. viruses 128, **128**
  blue eyes 96, **96**
  cheese made from bacteria 27, **27**
  feet 27, **27,** 31, 59, **59**
  medical treatments 116, 121, **121,** 142
  mites 102, **102**
  mucus 126
  in museum displays 170
  skeleton 8–9, **8–9**
  taste buds 31
  vein vs. artery 72, **72**
Humpback whales 180–181, **180–181**
Hyenas 75

I

Ice caps 88
Ice hotel 111, **111**
Icebergs 73, **73**
Iceland 171
Igneous rocks 164
IMAX cameras 175, **175**
Immortal jellyfish **86–87,** 87
Impalas 74
Indonesia 79, **79,** 144–145, **144–145**
Insects
  Amazon rainforest 6, **6**
  bug facts 58–61, **58–61**
  vs. arachnids vs. bugs 12, **12**
  wasp vs. hornet vs. bee 164
International Pillow Fight Day 106, **106**
International Space Station 10–11, **10–11,** 67, **67,** 152
Internet history 65
Inventions 48–49, **48–49**
Iron 90
Istanbul, Turkey 50, 170, **170**

J

Jackfruit 178
Jacks (game) 37, **37**
Jackson, Andrew 27
Jacques, David 94
Jaguars 129, **129**
Jakarta, Indonesia 56, 144
Jaws (movie) 174, **174**
Jay-Z 153, **153**

Jefferson, Thomas 46, 151
Jellyfish **86–87,** 87, 97, **97,** 115
Jigsaw puzzles 151
John, Elton 153, **153**
Johnson, Lyndon B. 177, **177**
Jupiter (planet) 122, **122**

K

Kanagawa, Japan 93, **93**
Kangaroos **124,** 125
Kawah Ijen volcano, Indonesia 144–145, **144–145**
Kennedy, John F. 176
Kepler space telescope 11
Kestrels 113
Kimchi 30, **30**
Kings and queens 132–133, **132–133**
Klondike gold rush 136
Knievel, Evel 52, **52**
Koalas 125, **125**
Koko (gorilla) 154
Krakatau, Indonesia 144

L

Lacrosse 72, **72**
Ladybugs 58, **58**
Lakes 88–89, **88–89**
Latvia 92
Legends 12, **12,** 94
Legos 36, **36**
Leonardo da Vinci 49, **49,** 72
Leopard seals 19
Leopards 75, 129, **129**
Lewis, Meriwether 151
Licklider, J. C. R. 65
Lighthouse hotel 111, **111**
Lights 92–93, **92–93**
Lincoln, Abraham 177
Lind, James 39
Lions 75, **75,** 154, **154**
Little blue penguins 146, **146**
Lizards 138
London, England
    Shard (skyscraper) 57, **57**
    soccer banned 119
    traffic light tree 159, **159**
    Transformer Statue 55, **55**
Londonderry, Annie 160
The Lord of the Rings 132
Los Glaciares National Park, Argentina **44–45,** 45

M

Madame Ching Shih (pirate) 104
Maglev trains 162
Mammoth Cave National Park, Kentucky, U.S.A. 44
Manatee Springs State Park, Florida, U.S.A. 89
Mandarin oranges 164
Mantella frogs 25, **25**
Maple syrup 68, **68**
Mardi Gras 46, **46**
Margarine 128, **128**
Margrethe II, Queen (Denmark) 132, **132**
Mariana Trench, Pacific Ocean 52
Marine mammals 18–19, **18–19**
Marksmen's Parade, Hanover, Germany 46
Mars (planet)
    astronaut journey to 71
    canyons 52
    rock formations 2
    rocks crashing into Earth 123
    rovers 11, **11**
Matsu Islands, Taiwan 97
Maya 141
McCartney, Paul 152, **152**
McDonald's 35, **35,** 160, **160**
McKinley, William 176
Megacities 56–57, **56–57**
Melissani Lake, Greece **88–89,** 89
Mendeleev, Dmitri 91, **91**
Mercury, Freddie 152
Metamorphic rocks 164, **164**
Meteorites 120, **120**
Mexico
    Aztec capital 57
    hot-air balloon festival 158, **158**
    pyramids 32, **32,** 140, **140–141**
Mice 33, **33**
Migration 74, **74,** 130–131, **130–131**
Milky Way galaxy 122, **122**
Miller, Bartshé 40
Mimic octopuses 117
Mir space station 34
Miranda, Lin-Manuel 153
Mites 102, **102**
M&M's 97, **97**
Mollusks 81, **81**
Monarch butterflies **130–131,** 131
Money 81, 91, **91**
Mongolia 79, **79**
Mono Lake, California, U.S.A. 2, **2–3,** 40, **41**
Monopoly game 35
Montezuma (Aztec ruler) 30
Moon 91, **91,** 96
Moonrats 100
Morris, Daisy 157
Moscow, Russia 92
Mosquitoes 59, 142, 171
Moths 58, **58**
Motorcycles 163, **163**
Mount Trashmore, Iowa, U.S.A. 148
Mountain gorillas **44**
Movies 174–175, **174–175**
Mr. Potato Head 35, **35**
Mucus 115, 126
Mudpuppies 23
Mumbai, India 57, **57**
Mushrooms 120, **120**
Music 39, **39,** 81, 152–153, **152–153**
Mussels 142
Myths 12, **12,** 156

N

National Security Agency 34
Nautiluses 42, **42**
Nectar 72, 101
Neptune (planet) 122
Netherlands 67
New Orleans, Louisiana, U.S.A. 46, **46**

New Year celebrations 46, **46–47**
New York City, U.S.A.
buses 162
Central Park 45
Christmas tree 92
facts 56, **56**
lighthouse hotel 111, **111**
Macy's Thanksgiving Day Parade 46
Newts 24, **24,** 25, **25,** 178
Nike shoes 69
Nile River, Africa 88
Nixon, Richard 154
Nocturnal animals 100–101, **100–101**
North Carolina, U.S.A. 136, **136**
Northern lights 14, **14–15,** 111
Norway 171, **171**
Nuclear submarines 39, **39**
Nuts 27, **27**

O

Obama, Barack 153
Octopuses 42–43, **42–43,** 81, **81,** 117
Okapis 167, **167**
Olympic games 67, **67,** 133, **133**
O'Neal, Shaquille 20
Opossums 101, 177, **177**
Optical illusions 158, **158**
Oranges 69, **69,** 164, **164**
Oreo cookies 98, **98**
Ostriches 63, 164
Otters 18, **18**
Owls
barn owls 100, **100,** 113
eyes 112, **112–113**
great horned owls 113
regurgitation 103, **103**
Oysters 80

P

Pacific beetle cockroaches 59, **59**
Pacific hagfish 103, **103**
Palaces 132, **132,** 133, **133**
Pancakes 68, 69
Pandas, giant 154, **154**
Parades
bicycle parade 67
costumes 54, **54**
facts 46, **46–47**
flower parade 158, **158**
Parker Pearson, Mike 94
Parker Solar Probe 11
Parks and preserves 44–45, **44–45**
Parrots 157, **157,** 176, **176**
Parton, Dolly 153, **153**
Peanut-head bugs 6, **6**
Penguins 146–147, **146–147,** 171, **171**
Peppers 30, **30,** 31, 106, **106**
Peregrine falcons 113
Periodic Table of Elements 90, 91
Perseverance (Mars rover) 11
Peru 140
Peter Pan (book and movie) 59, **59**
Piano fangblenny 115
Pigs 62, 63, 167
Pirate facts 104–105, **104–105**
Pitcher plants 82, **82,** 83
Planets vs. stars 13, **13**
Plants
carnivorous 82–83, **82–83**
defenses 28, **28–29**
flowers 79, **79,** 178, **178**
trees 50, **50,** 69, 78
Plastics
arts and crafts from 149, **149**
eaten by bacteria 50
filtered from waterways 51
future 71
Play-Doh 34, **34**
Plot, Robert 161
Pluto (dwarf planet) 122
Poison frogs 23, 25, **25**
Polar bears 19, **19,** 133, **133**
Pollen 72
Ponies 177
Poop
animal defenses 138, **138**
covering eggs 103
eaten by dung beetles 102, **102**
eaten by tilapia fish 155
electricity from 51
feeding plants 83
fossilized 121, 156
insect poop 61
seen from space 146
sloths 84, 85
Porcupines 72, 138, **138,** 178, **178**
Porpoises 18
Port Royal, Jamaica 104
Portland, Oregon, U.S.A. 51
Portuguese man-of-war 97, **97**
Potato beetles 138
Potatoes 54, **54**
Pottos 178
Predator facts 76–77, **76–77,** 112–113, **112–113**
Presidents *see* White House, Washington, D.C., U.S.A.
Presley, Elvis 46, **46,** 153, **153**
Pricey facts 120–121
Prickly pear cactus 178, **178**
Prince (musician) 152
Pterosaurs 157
Pufferfish **178–179,** 179
Puzzles and codes 150–151, **150–151**
Pyramids 32, **32,** 140–141, **140–141,** 164, **164**

Q

Qal'at Mgouna, Morocco 46
Queens and kings 132–133, **132–133**
Quokkas 125, **125**

R

Raccoons 101, **101,** 176, **176**
Recycling 50, **50,** 148–149, **148–149,** 158, **158**
Red-tailed hawks 113
Regurgitation (vomit) 59, **59,** 103, 167
Restaurants, sky-high 106, **106**
Rhinos 74
Rio de Janeiro, Brazil 46, 92, **92**
Rivers 88–89

Roads 51, **51**
Robots
biomimicry 142
future 71, **71**
RoboCup competition 118, **118**
robotic dinosaur at hotel 111, **111**
space 11, **11**
vs. androids 72, **72**
Rock formations 2, **2-3,** 15, 40, **41**
Rock types 164, **164**
Rome, ancient 32, 91, 151, **151**
Roof shingles 51
Roosevelt, Archie 177
Roosevelt, Theodore 177
Rose Bowl Parade, Pasadena, California, U.S.A. 46, **46**
Rose butterflies 143, **143**
Rubik's Cube 36, **36,** 150, **150**
Rulers (kings and queens) 132-133, **132-133**
Ruppell's griffon vultures 112

S

Saint Paul, Minnesota, U.S.A. 46
Salamanders 22, **22,** 23, 24, 83, **83**
Salt 91
San Francisco 49ers 137, **137**
São Paulo, Brazil 56
Sasquatch 128
Satsuma mandarins 164
Scorpions 121, **121**
Scrimshaw 38, **38**
Scurvy 39
Sea cucumbers 138, **138**
Sea hares 126, **126**
Sea urchins 178
Seahorses 115, **115**
Seals 18, 19, 88, **88,** 172-173, **172-173**
Seashells 80-81, **80-81**
Seasons 32-33, **32-33**
Secret codes 150-151, **150-151**
Sedimentary rocks 164
Sequoias 15
Serebrov, Aleksandr 34
Serengeti animals 74-75, **74-75**
Shanghai, China 56, **56-57**
Sheep **62-63,** 63, 176
Shells 80-81, **80-81**
Sherbet 12, **12**
Ships 38-39, **38-39**
Shoes 20, **20,** 69, 148, **148-149**
Siberian newts 24, **24**
Silly Putty 37
Silveira, Regina 158, **158**
Skeleton, human 8-9, **8-9**
Sleet 128
Slinkys 36, **36**
Sloths 84-85, **84-85**
Slugs 126, **126**
Snakes
Australia 125, **125**
black king snakes 76
cake shaped like 54, **54**
migration 130, **130**
world's heaviest 7
Snow leopards 76
Soap 49, **49**
Soccer 21, **21,** 43, 118-119, **118-119**
Sodium 91, **91**
Solar cells 143
Solar system facts 122-123, **122-123**
Sorbet 12, **12**
Sounds
birds of prey 113
Chichen Itza, Mexico 141, **141**
facts 16-17, **16-17**
northern lights 14
soccer 119
Victoria Falls, Zambia-Zimbabwe 14
Space
black holes 108-109, **108-109**
fruit flies in 59
helium rockets 91
holiday lights seen from 92
moon landing 91
music concert 152
poop seen from 146
solar system facts 122-123, **122-123**
star vs. planet 13, **13**
Space shuttle 11, 65
Spacecraft facts 10-11, **10-11**
SpaceX 11
Spanish ribbed newts 178
Sperm whales 18
Spicy foods 30-31, **30-31**
Spiders 76, **76, 138-139,** 139
Spinning tops 37, **37**
Split Apple Rock (Tokangawhā), New Zealand 15, **15**
Sponges 115, 116, 117, **117**
Sports
baseball 128, 168-169, **168-169**
basketball 20-21, **20-21**
cricket 128, **128**
field hockey vs. lacrosse 72, **72**
Olympic games 133, **133**
pancake race 68
San Francisco 49ers 137, **137**
soccer 21, **21,** 43, 118-119, **118-119**
see also Bicycles
Spring 32
Squid 42
Sriracha hot sauce 31, **31**
St. Helens, Mount, Washington, U.S.A. 16
St. Patrick's Day 46
Stalactites 165, **165**
Stalagmites 165, **165**
Star Wars 52, 58, 158, **158**
Stars vs. planets 13, **13**
Sticky facts 126-127, **126-127,** 142, 143, **143**
Stonehenge, England 94-95, **94-95**
"Straw bears" outfit 107, **107**
Straw-colored fruit bats 131, **131**
Strel, Martin 89
Submarines 39, **39,** 48, **48**
Subways 57, **57,** 162, **162**
Sudan 140, 141, **141**
Sulfur 145
Summer 32
Summer solstice 92
Sun 11, 109, **109,** 122
Sundew plants 83, **83**
Super Soaker 37
Swans 133
Swift, Taylor 152, **152**

Swiftlet nests 121, **121**
Sydney, Australia 46, **46-47**

T

Taaffeite gem 120, **120**
Tadpoles 23, **23**
Taft, William 177
Taj Mahal, Agra, India 78, **78**
Tangerines 164, **164**
Tapirs 167, **167**
Tarantulas **138-139,** 139
Tarsiers 100, **100**
Taste buds 31
Tea 121, **121,** 170, **170**
Teeth 9, **9,** 26, **26**
Termites 61, **61,** 142, **142**
Terns 130, **130**
Tetris 34, **34**
Text messages 161
Thistles 178, **178**
Three Gorges Dam, China 89
Tic-tac-toe 151, **151**
Tilapia fish 155
Titicaca, Lake 89
Toads 23, **23,** 24, **24,** 25, **25**
Toco toucans 6, **6**
Tokyo, Japan 57, 106, **106,** 111, **111**
Tongue-eating louse 103, **103**
Tooting 103
Tortoises 15, **15**
Toucans 6, **6**
Tour de France 66, **66**
Toys & games 34-37, **34-37,** 150-151, **150-151**
Traffic signals 49, **49,** 159, **159**
Trains 162, **162,** 163
Transformers (movie) 55
Transportation *see* Vehicle facts
Trash into treasure 148-149, **148-149**
Travel, future 70
Trees 50, **50,** 69, 78
Trekking 12, **12**
Tromsø, Norway 33
Truffles 120, **120**
Tsukioka, Aya 106
Tsunamis 104, 142
Tube-lipped nectar bats 101, **101**
Tufa towers 2, **2-3,** 40, **41**
Turtles 115
Tutankhamun, King 37, 133, **133**
Tyrannosaurus rex 63, 156

U

Uranus (planet) 33

V

Vanilla beans 120, **120**
Vehicle facts 162-163, **162-163**
  see also Airplanes; Bicycles; Cars; Subways
Veins 72, **72**
Velcro 126, **126**
Venus flytraps **82-83,** 83
Victoria Falls, Zambia-Zimbabwe 14
Video games 63, 118
Vietnam War 36
Viking longships 38, **38-39**
Virunga National Park, Democratic Republic of the Congo 44, **44**
Viruses 128, **128**
Vlad III Dracula 132, **132**
Volcanoes 16, 125, 144-145, **144-145**
Vomit (regurgitation) 59, **59,** 103, 167
Voyager 1 spacecraft 11
Voynich manuscript 151, **151**
Vultures 112, 113, **113**

W

Wall, Rachel and George 105
Wallace and Gromit (cartoon characters) 27, **27**
Walruses 18, **18-19**
Washington, D.C., U.S.A. 93, **93**
  see also White House, Washington, D.C., U.S.A.
Washington, George 151
Wasps 58, 138, 164
Water buffalo 12, **12**
Water conservation 51, **51**
Watermelons, as skis 125
Whales
  beluga whales 18, **18**
  blue whales 19, **19,** 76
  as hippo relatives 167
  humpback whales 180-181, **180-181**
  sperm whales 18
  teeth 38, **38**
White House, Washington, D.C., U.S.A.
  cheese 27, **27**
  electric lights 161, **161**
  entertainment 153
  Fourth of July parade 46
  movie theater 174, **174**
  pets 176-177, **176-177**
Wildebeest 74, **74**
Wilson, Woodrow 176
Wind 15, 122
Winter 33
Wolverine frogs 138
Wolves 76, **76-77**
Woodhull, Victoria 161, **161**
World War II 35, 128, 150
Wright, Orville and Wilbur 66, 160

Y

Yarlung Tsangpo Grand Canyon, Tibet 53
Yellowstone National Park, U.S.A. 45, **45**
Yeti 128, **128**
Yurts 79, **79**

Z

Zebras 74, **74-75,** 167
Zimbabwe 142
Zooplankton 131
Zoos 51, 154-155, **154-155**

For Diane, the most fantastic mom —JB

For BHG, JRG, and GEG —MRH

For Zoomer, the world's weirdest cat —AH

Copyright © 2023 National Geographic Partners, LLC

All rights reserved. Reproduction of the whole or any part of the contents without written permission from the publisher is prohibited.

NATIONAL GEOGRAPHIC and Yellow Border Design are trademarks of the National Geographic Society, used under license.

Since 1888, the National Geographic Society has funded more than 14,000 research, conservation, education, and storytelling projects around the world. National Geographic Partners distributes a portion of the funds it receives from your purchase to National Geographic Society to support programs including the conservation of animals and their habitats. To learn more, visit natgeo.com/info.

For more information, visit nationalgeographic.com, call 1-877-873-6846, or write to the following address:

National Geographic Partners, LLC
1145 17th Street NW
Washington, DC 20036-4688 U.S.A.

For librarians and teachers: nationalgeographic.com/books/librarians-and-educators

More for kids from National Geographic: natgeokids.com

National Geographic Kids magazine inspires children to explore their world with fun yet educational articles on animals, science, nature, and more. Using fresh storytelling and amazing photography, *Nat Geo Kids* shows kids ages 6 to 14 the fascinating truth about the world—and why they should care.
natgeo.com/subscribe

For rights or permissions inquiries, please contact National Geographic Books Subsidiary Rights: bookrights@natgeo.com

Designed by Chad Tomlinson

The publisher would like to thank Julie Beer, Michelle Harris, and Avery Hurt, authors and researchers; Grace Hill Smith, project manager; Emily Fego, project editor; Alison O'Brien Muff, photo editor; Lori Epstein, photo director; Amanda Larsen, art director; Julide Dengel, senior designer; Jennifer Geddes, fact-checker; Vivian Suchman, managing editor; Molly Reid, production editor; and Anne LeongSon and Gus Tello, associate designers.

Hardcover ISBN: 978-1-4263-7225-4
Reinforced library binding ISBN: 978-1-4263-7226-1

Printed in Hong Kong
22/PPHK/1